# KING TULLE

## THE FOUNDING OF TULABORG

*By the same author*

THE UNICORN (Lutterworth Press, London)
THE MAHARAJAH ADVENTURE (Lutterworth Press, London)
GOLDCROWN LANE (Oxford University Press, Oxford)
THE GOLDMAKER'S HOUSE (Oxford University Press, Oxford)
HORSES OF THE NIGHT (Oxford University Press, Oxford)

Irmelin Sandman Lilius

# KING TULLE

## THE FOUNDING OF TULABORG

Translated by JOAN TATE

PELHAM BOOKS

To Carl-Gustaf

First published in Great Britain by
Pelham Books Ltd
44 Bedford Square
London WC1B 3DU
1980

First published as *Kung Tulle* by
Bonnier and Schildt, Sweden and Finland
1972



ISBN 0 7207 1192 4

Filmset and printed in Great Britain by
BAS Printers Limited, Over Wallop, Hampshire

# CONTENTS

# I

# KING TULLE

King Tulle was the son of old King Sigulf, who ruled over the long green valleys round the River Sigga. King Tulle himself acquired a kingdom further west. That was after Sigulf had died, and Tulle himself was banished by his half-brothers, who were bigger and stronger than he was.

The brothers had three different mothers, and had never been friends. The elder was called Steinhulf and the second Bork. They beat Tulle with staves, calling him Lout-Tulle and a changeling. They said they had no wish to see him any longer.

Tulle was nothing but a boy at the time, lanky and thin, his fair hair falling over his eyes, his manner slow. He looked at his brothers standing there before him with their staves and said that he would willingly go, but before he did, he wished to receive his heritage from his mother, which consisted of twelve goats.

Steinhulf bawled that he would not get as much as a single goat-dropping. Tulle stood still, but an expression came into his eyes that perhaps frightened Bork, or perhaps filled him with compassion or annoyance with Steinhulf, who always wanted to decide everything. In the end, Tulle was given his goats, and away he drove them into the forest.

It was early spring. The grass had hardly begun to grow, but birds were singing everywhere. The goats leapt about, making it difficult for him to keep them in order. Tulle was fairly happy in himself, but he hurried on westwards as fast as he could, almost expecting his brothers to change their minds, to follow him and try to kill him.

When evening came, he tied the goats' legs together to keep them quiet, then milked them. They gave little enough milk after the long winter, but he squeezed a few drops from each, then lit a fire and sat by it to keep watch through the night.

As he sat tending the fire and listening in the damp twilight, he made himself a horn from alder-bark.

After he had travelled far away to the west and south-west, he came to a clump of rounded hills. He stopped on the highest of them and looked round. He had come to the edge of the sea, where a river ran into the sea, and it was green and beautiful and uninhabited, no smoke as far as could be seen. Then he put the horn to his lips and blew into it. Tooo-hooo. And all his goats came tumbling down the slope.

Thus the country on the edge of the sea became his, stretching as far as the sound of his horn.

Tooo-hooo on the horn
twelve beasts, they were
twelve names, they had
far, far they wandered
and found a new land
the king himself their goatherd. . .

He called the country Tuntula and himself King Tulle. At first he thought of settling on the rivermouth, but it was marshy there. So he chose a point further out, on the eastern bank, where he was protected by water on three sides and had good dry foundations to build on. He made a brushwood hut for the goats and himself, but even on that first night he dreamt of great houses and halls. When he woke, he said: 'This will be my domain and its name shall be Tulaborg.'

Then he crept out of the hairy flea-ridden warmth of the goats into the grey dew.

The sun had not yet risen, the grass cold, the air cold, the sky almost white. From every direction, from every tree, birdsong leapt and showered and trembled, and the shining water ahead of him was spotted with sea-birds and the heads of seals. Above the constant screaming of gulls, he could hear the a- a- a-oo-lee call of the long-tailed duck and the hollow ooo a-ooo of the eider. Possessed by his new happiness, shivering, hungry and happy, he leapt down the slope and into the water.

As he puffed and swam and worked up a foam, his

subjects the goats came tripping with small steps out of the shed, the forelegs fettered to their back legs with pieces of rope so that they could not run away.

He also built a fence as soon as he could, right across the headland of Tulaborg hill, clearing the forest in a broad belt beyond it. But he had constant trouble all the same. He could stop the goats getting out, but not the beasts of the forest getting in, if he did not keep an eye out for them all the time. There were bears and wolves, foxes and lynxes, and rustling hordes of smaller creatures, troll-creatures and nameless creepy-crawlies.

For the country was full of forces that he either had to frighten away or keep in with. Tulle did not know much about such things, but he did his best. He blew on his horn and shot burning arrows, and when he found the spring on the southern hillside, he was very polite to the water-spirits living in it. He bowed and spoke with dignity, and to make sure, he also gave them his only ornament, the silver clasp that held his tunic together at the neck.

One night, the wind turned and began to blow from the south-west. At first it felt warm, but soon it was drawing the mist out of the sea, and that mist was thick and raw, penetrating everything, so that the goats became dejected and Tulle himself depressed and low-spirited.

When three days had gone by without a sign of the sun, it was almost as if winter had returned. He shivered in his hut, which the goats almost filled, wet and smelling strongly, and whatever he did, he could not get the fire to burn, because he had run out of kindling. He had shot a merganser a while before, and had the carcass left, a mess of bones and scorched scraps. He sucked at it until it sickened him and then flung it outside. Then he began to think about eggs.

Because he had been forced to watch over the goats all the time, and had been unable to explore his kingdom or even decide on the boundaries, it extended only as far as he could see. Now, in the three-day mist, it had grown quite small, and grey, too, so that it seemed ancient and disintegrated. He too, felt old and wretched. But he thought that if only he could have an egg to eat, then things would change. The sun-shaped yolk would warm his whole body and make him strong and brave again. Two eggs, or three, would brighten the whole day.

The more he thought about it, the worse his hunger became, and the knowledge that there really were eggs for the taking, as many as he liked, on the rocky shores and out on the islands, made him restless. The sea-birds nested close together out there. He had heard and seen that on the very first day, but had not dared go out there, either swimming with a log or with a brushwood raft, because he dared not leave the goats alone for so long.

He looked at them with indignation as his mouth watered more and more. If he had not insisted on taking them with him, he could have explored all day long. He could have lived on the islands and eaten himself quite yellow with eggs. But he had to admit that without his goats, he would not have been king at all, only a simple forest-runner.

The goats were lying quite quietly in the hut. The fence was sturdy and high, and the smell of smoke that kept the forest beasts at bay lay heavily over the whole of the hillside. He decided to risk it, just to the nearest rocky shore.

It was just as he had thought down there, plenty of nests. But while he was leaping round collecting a few eggs from each nest, making a hole in the shell and sucking them in more and more happily, two men came to Tulaborg. Their names were Sote and Laff, and they had been sent by the kings of Sigga Valley to find and kill Tulle and to retrieve the goats. Cautiously, they peered over the fence, and when they saw that only the goats were at home, they climbed over it and slaughtered one of the goats, the one Tulle called Blackie. They lit a fire – they had tinder and kindling with them – and began to roast the meat. They did not have permission from the kings to do this but they thought that when they returned to Sigga Valley, they would say that Tulle had had only eleven goats left.

The mist remained just as thick all the time, and while Tulle was collecting eggs, he had birds and bird-cries constantly swirling round his head. But when he came down on to the shore again, other sounds penetrated. He heard his goats bleating and realized from the note that they were afraid. He had hauled his tunic out from his stomach, so that it hung like a pouch over his belt, and he had stowed the eggs he could not eat into the pouch. Now he hurried off homewards, leaping from stone to stone, careful not to damage the eggs.

The goats were standing right down by the water, huddled against the fence and half-clambering on top of one another. They surged round him when he approached, and he had to shove them away with his hands and knees. At once, he saw that Blackie was missing, and as he came up the slope, the smell of roast meat filled his nostrils.

He was moving lightly and cautiously, and caught sight of Sote and Laff sitting by the fire before they noticed him. He recognized them, and when he saw how well armed they were, he guessed what they had come for. They had swords and spears, and leather coats with wooden strips stitched to them, their helmets on the ground by the fire.

He drew back and thought for a moment about what he should do. His bow and arrows were inside the hut, but he had his knife in his hand.

He cut the ropes binding the goats' legs and drove them at the fire, spurring them on with the tip of his knife and making them gallop, bleating wildly. Sote and Laff jumped to their feet, their swords drawn and their necks outstretched as they peered in amongst the trees, but Tulle circled round them and came up from behind, where his store of timber and wood lay drying. He picked up a pine branch, trimmed and smooth to hold, curved and thick at the end. Sote was standing with his helmet in his hand, about to put it on.

Tulle gripped his knife between his teeth and grasped the branch with both hands. Then he leapt forward, striking Sote on the back of the head with all his might. Sote fell. But Laff hurled himself forward, slashing at Tulle with his sword. Tulle flung up his branch and the sword fastened into it, twisting it out of his hand.

Laff was strong, raising the sword with the branch wedged into it, and Tulle leapt back, thrust his hand into the pouch in his tunic, took an egg and hurled it straight at Laff's face.

He threw egg after egg, blinding Laff, and before Laff had time to wipe his eyes, Tulle had jumped on him with his knife and thrust it in just below his ear. Laff let out a gurgling bellow, and thrashed about with his arms and legs. Tulle snatched up Sote's sword and hacked off Laff's head as quickly as he could. Then he hacked off Sote's head, too, to make sure. Then he sat down for a rest.

He wept a little when he saw Blackie's flayed carcass lying on the ground, the eyelashes still there round the yellow eyes. But then he turned the wooden spit round so that the meat threaded on to it would not burn.

When he looked up again, a tiny figure was just climbing over the fence. He could not see very clearly, as the figure was as grey as the mist itself. But he was more frightened of it than he had been of Sote and Laff, so frightened that it was as if his blood were turning black. He picked up the sword again, but found himself unable to hold it steady.

But the goats had stopped bleating and all of them came trotting back together.

'Don't worry about me,' said the figure. 'You'll recognize me if you look hard enough. I'm neither ghost nor troll. I followed Sote and Laff into the forest, and I thought I'd go ahead of them and warn you. But I fell behind, as I had such a heavy bundle to carry.'

It was an old woman, as small as a child, and a hunchback. Her hair was short and blowing round her brown face, her eyes glittering like water when she smiled. Tulle dropped the sword and attempted to laugh, but his breath was trembling in his throat, yes, his body was trembling all over, so that he was unable to rise to his feet. He had known this little old woman all his life. She had looked after him when he was small and he had lived with her in a turf hut on the edge of the king's domain for several years. She was called Halva, because she was half the size of a person, and because she was so small, people did not really know what kind of being she was. There were many who thought that a ghost or a troll was exactly what she was.

'I'm not afraid,' said Tulle, and that was true now that he had recognized her. 'But I feel weak and ill,' he went on. 'Perhaps I ate too many eggs. I was down on the shore collecting eggs when they came.'

She looked at him with her pale eyes and then said: 'That's not the eggs.' She was gazing at him so searchingly that he felt abashed and looked down. Then when he caught sight of the bodies and heads lying there, he felt better again.

'My brothers don't think much of me, do they?' he said. 'Sending only two men for me.'

'They'll probably send more when Sote and Laff don't return.'

He did not know what to say to that, and neither did he really know what to do next. The mist was as thick and grey as ever and the trees looked like dark grey birds, all standing still on one sturdy leg, the other drawn up and hidden beneath them. But they could also have been grey warriors who had surrounded him and captured him there on the hill.

'When I struck them down, I forgot that he who falls stays there,' said Tulle. 'Will they walk again? Will they climb over the fence every night all over again?'

Perhaps he could take the goats on a raft over to the islands and live there? Ghosts could walk on water, of course. But he would be protected from ordinary men from Sigga Valley for a long time. He said so to Halva and she nodded, but did not reply. The fire crackled. The meat was cooked now and smelt good.

He thought he would not eat until he had decided whether he would stay or go. But while he was still hesitating, he heard a whimpering sound from over by the fence. He went over to see what it was, and there was the large homespun bundle that Halva had left on the other side. Three small pups were trying to crawl out of its folds.

He lifted over both bundle and pups, and the pups trembled and licked him, trying to chew the tunic that was soiled down the front with egg.

'They're for you,' said Halva. 'They're from a litter a bitch of your mother's had.'

Tulle was pleased. He said nothing, but the corners of his mouth turned up towards his ears. He went to fetch water in his bark-pail, took the meat off the fire and placed it on a flat stone. Then he bade Halva help herself. He cut small strips of it for the pups, and after they had eaten and noisily drunk some water, they started yapping and playing about, nipping at the back legs of the goats until they kicked out, at which the pups quickly retreated, complaining and seeking protection with Halva. After a while, all three pups fell asleep in a heap by the fire. Tulle ate slowly, the misty trees now resembling his own faithful guards. Without further consideration, he decided to stay and accept the fate intended for him, here on the hill that was his royal domain.

They did not have to wait long for the next man from Sigga Valley. Only a few days later, as Tulle was coming up the hillside with a bundle of fish – he had been down to strip his fishing-lines – he heard voices. And he stopped behind the new hut he had made on stilts to keep his clothes and weapons out of reach of the pups and goats.

'I said so. I said that two was too few,' an old voice was chuckling. 'I remember the Signs when he was born. I remember the Red Star in the south over the sea. I told them they wouldn't get him. I told them to turn back. But they just laughed and went off with their rotten brown swords. I told them to remember what I'd said when he struck them down. And I saw their heads on those stakes as I came over the hill. It's nice to know I was right. I laughed and waved as I went by. But what've you done with their bodies, then?'

'Sunk them in the marsh down there,' said Halva.

'I hope you remembered to stake them well? I remember what happened when Laxake was killed, and he didn't stay down long, that he didn't. On the fourth day, or perhaps it was the fifth, he came up again – did you put flowers over them? It's important to have at least some kind of flowers.'

'You needn't remind me about such things,' said Halva impatiently. 'We took their clothes and things, and wove wreaths and kirtles instead with that yellow marsh-grass and sallow – there aren't any other flowers at this time of year. And we've staked them down with oak-staves and juniper-hooks, so they'll stay down, if a few stakes and hooks mean anything.'

The old man chuckled and clucked. 'I knew it. I knew you'd gone after them. I went to see you one evening about this crooked leg of mine, to ask you to rub it a little in that way you have, and you'd gone, and all your jars were gone, too – tell me, what've you done with all your jars?'

'Have you followed me all those miles through the forest for me to rub your rickety old shank? Or was it just inquisitiveness?'

There was a chuckle. 'You see right through me, you do, and you hear what's meant right through what a man says. No one can fool you, that they can't, and I knew that, too . . . No,' the old voice went on, suddenly secretive and low. 'I came because there's war coming down there in Sigga Valley. Our kings have divided the kingdom into the East Half and West Half and they're supposed to be friends. But they're already greedily eyeing each other's halves. I came because I know and I remember the Signs from above heaven and earth when this Tulle was born. He'll be the most renowned of the brothers yet, he'll be the greatest. His honour will last as long as his country stands, even when it has burnt down, and even when the black sea has drowned it – I came because I'd rather follow him than be against him, and you did so, too, otherwise you wouldn't have slunk away here . . .'

'Hobard, your mind is wandering. I came for quite another reason. You wouldn't understand, even if I tried to tell you. I haven't time for all your talk now. You must wait until he comes back and talk to him yourself. Perhaps he'll let you stay.'

Tulle came out from behind the hut and the old man with his whining voice turned and bowed, holding his hands on his chest. He screwed up his eyes and chuckled: 'Oh, how he's grown. And no doubt he'll grow all the more . . . I've come to enter your service, King Tulle.'

Tulle thought for a moment and then said: 'You can be my fisherman.'

Then a troop came from King Steinhulf, sent to kill King Tulle, and on the way they met a troop King Bork had sent on the same errand. Both fought each other until only three men were left. The three wounded men crawled down to Tulaborg and asked to join King Tulle. At the time, he was busy clearing the fields to sow buckwheat and turnips with the seed Halva had brought with her in the bundle. He let her take care of the men and tend to their wounds, and he had Hobard make a hut for them.

He thought about the great house he would build one day, and he went round selecting timber that he barked and left standing to dry.

The grass was growing now, the trees in leaf, and everything was so beautiful, he did not know which way to look. There was plenty of food. Every evening, they set snares for birds and hares. They collected eggs and made a windsock out of a capercaillie tail on a stake. They gathered eggs and edible grasses and tapped sap from the birches.

The goats almost all had kids, and the pups slowly learnt to herd them.

When the three wounded men were well again, they were sent up into the forest to retrieve the weapons and clothes of the men who had killed each other and still lay up there; a king needed stores and had to be able to support his people. For his people were becoming more and more numerous now.

Refugees came from Sigga Valley with their servants and animals, wind-driven fishermen came from the sea, forest-runners came alone, all asking for protection from King Tulle. Within a few years, he was king of a hundred or so people, and most of them thought he was a good king, although he was so young.

He was quite handsome, too. He never grew tall, but he was strong and well-built. His eyes were oval-shaped, large and bluish-greenish grey, his hair fair and curly at the ears, his nose straight and short, his mouth wide, his teeth as strong as a seal's.

## 2

# THE TROLLS

Right from the start, Tulaborg had been troubled by trolls. They could be seen and heard in the forest, coming closer at dusk and at night and standing sniffing the air from the meadows.

There they were, those huge creatures hurling boulders as large as horses and cows and whole houses, but fortunately usually missing. Most of the boulders flung at Tulaborg went too far, flying over the water and falling onto the nearest island, so that sparks flew from the rocks. Such a rubble of rocks and scree gathered there that the island was given the name Rummel Island, which means Rubble Island.

There were smaller trolls, too, that turned aside with bowed backs if they met anyone, tucking in their tails and slinking away. There was also a little grey kind that stole milk from the cattle, and a tiny little kind that was hairy, bright yellow or black, that lived off honey. And there were trolls of the brooding kind that had been sitting still for so long that moss had grown over them, as well as over whole great trees.

There were many more kinds of trolls, and gnomes,

dwarfs and spirits, many more than in Sigga Valley, and some were hard to tell from animals and shadows and tangled roots, if anyone came across them unexpectedly in the forest.

King Tulle built the hall he had imagined, but it took many years to complete. That first summer, he built ordinary dwelling-houses and cattle-sheds with gables of timber and long walls of turf and stone. For roofing, he used bark stripped in the summer, four layers of it, and on top a double layer of fresh turf, the lower layer with the grass turned downwards. Such a roof lasted for a generation. The turf grew and withered with the seasons, making the houses difficult to distinguish at a distance, resembling oblong hillocks, and snowdrifts in the winter.

The hall was different. It was built very high, for a start. The roof supports were in two rows, from gable to gable and all made of selected redwood. Spurs and trusses were from naturally curved trees, the strongest available. The hearth was long and narrow and ran down the middle of the floor, and a smoke-hatch was made in the roof. Sleeping places were made between the pillars and walls, the entrance in the middle of the eastern gable. At the western end, Tulle constructed his throne-platform, and he made the throne itself from a pine tree that had grown crooked and divided itself into several trunks. He hollowed out the fork and made it into a seat, and on the trunks stretching up towards the roof, he carved figures of people and animals. He carved no images, but all the signs and symbols of the gods: sun-wheels and wind-ensigns for the Lord of the Skies, who had so many names, most of them too sacred to be uttered aloud. Tund or Tinderas he was called in everyday speech. And then the sign of the waves and fishing-signs for the Lord of the Sea, and an ear of corn and other plants for the Good Earth. And many many more.

Tulle's people had made themselves a sacred place on the hillside south of Tulaborg, where a spring rose and a few small pine trees stood bowed by the eternal wind from the sea. They hung flowers in the pines and went there when they wanted to talk or ask advice from those who were wiser and greater than man. Tulle's people had no special priests or holy men, but there were always a few, especially among the elders, who maintained they knew more than others about the wishes and habits of the gods, and who therefore thought that the people in general should also obey them.

Tulle carved runes too, and invented some of his own, when he considered existing ones were not good enough, or when he could not remember them. He took time and trouble to have everything well done, although constantly harassed by old Hobard, who fussed round him and knew better. Hobard made a lot of fuss about the throne platform.

In Sigga Valley, the throne platform had always been in the centre of one of the long walls with the seats of those next in rank opposite. But Tulle did not wish things to be like his brothers', as he had his own special individual kingly pride and wished to have things his own way.

Behind the throne was an additional structure, a chamber where he slept. It had a hatch door and a window in the roof, a tiny hole covered with the foetal membrane of a kid. This let in a soft light, but could not be seen through.

Old Hobard kept on and on about Tulle needing a crown. He said that if everyone's clasps and buckles and other ornaments were collected together, there would be enough for a headband. Hardly any of them had gold ornaments, but silver and copper and bronze would do. When Tulle said no to this, Hobard went on about a headband of iron, at least, offering to forge Sote's now rusty short-sword and set the teeth of the great bear they had killed the previous winter in it as decoration. Tulle said no rather sharply to this suggestion, too. Then one of the women half jokingly wove him a crown of narrow strips of birch-bark. It looked more like a bottomless basket, and when he saw it, he laughed. He put it on and found it light on his head. But he did not wear it very often, but let it hang on a projection on his throne.

The hall also had a turf roof, but Tulle made gable boards at the gables, crossed boards with dragon heads on them. They swallowed wind and spat rain and praised the sun. He had wanted to gild them, but had to be content with painting them red with elder-bark stain.

Perhaps it was the gaping dragon heads that stung the eyes of the great trolls and made them think of blood.

One day, when it was almost midsummer, the young herdsmen found it difficult to keep their creatures together. They blew on their horns and pipes and ran about sweating, but every time they got the herd together something came and frightened them again, sending them scattering in all directions and racing all the way up to Black Forest, their herdsmen following them, weary and almost in tears. They were three children, Kotkel and Egil and a girl called Hulda. And two dogs.

They came into the shadow below a large mountain, and at once, great boulders began flying round them, snapping off branches and whole trees, and a cow that the children had almost caught was struck down and lay bellowing on the ground. The children threw themselves down and crouched against the mountain wall. They had immediately realized that the trolls had come, and were so frightened that they could hardly move. But they wriggled face down under the thick bracken, the ground shaking so much that they felt it right through their bodies. The trolls came nearer, their thunderous voices echoing against the mountain-side.

'Is that you, my good-weather brother?' said one, laughing. 'I see that you are also a tormentor of people.'

'Of course,' came the reply from the darkness of the pines. 'You have to watch out for such miserable creeps before there are too many of them. I thought I'd managed to catch one,' said the troll, striding down. The children could see through the bracken that it was dressed in furs and heavily ornamented, its head hairy and unkempt and its eyes wild. It picked up a felled birch and began to strike the ground with it all round between the trees, its ears twitching, its nostrils and eyes flashing sharply from right to left.

The children lay still, clasping each other with icy hands. They did not move, although the troll was thrashing about so close to them that the birch-top brushed their legs.

'Come and help,' it said.

The other troll came closer and both of them stamped around for a while. They broke the back of the injured cow and then tore it to pieces with their bare hands. They gnawed and swallowed, and when they spoke again, it was with their mouths full of meat, so their speech was blurred and hard to understand. But all the same, this is what the children heard:

'It doesn't matter all that much, does it?' said one of them, chewing away.

'You have to watch it with these people,' the other replied. 'There aren't that many of them as yet, and I know some of us think they're funny to look at, but they breed faster than mice. They're settling on the coasts first, down on the shores, but soon there'll be enough of them that they'll start gnawing away the land. They've weapons we haven't got.'

'Isn't there enough land for all of us?'

'The country's ours. But if the people grow strong, they'll say it's theirs. I can already hear the greed humming in their round little skulls. I can smell something in their sweat that I'm afraid of . . .'

And where they lay the children heard the trolls coming to an agreement. They would gather their allies together and make for Tulaborg that very night. They would lift the roofs off the people's houses and bite the people's heads off, and they would trample every building into matchwood.

When the children came rushing home, mindless with terror and so out of breath that they could hardly get the words out of their mouths, their elders at once realized what had happened. Their mothers scolded them because they had neglected the cattle: some of the cows had come home on their own, but others had not come at all, and where were the dogs?

'The trolls! The trolls!' gasped the children, not caring about either mothers or cattle. 'Where's King Tulle?' Before anyone had time to answer, they saw him standing over by the hall. They rushed over to him, trembling with exhaustion, their breath wheezing and stinging in their throats. They were dirtier than usual, their faces streaked with tears, their linen tunics torn, and they were covered with bleeding scratches.

Tulle told them to calm down and get their breath back, but there was no time for that. Between hiccoughs and cries, they managed to get out that the trolls were on their way, the trolls were on their way!

Everyone who heard them began to rush about the place whimpering, some grabbed their weapons, but Tulle stood quite still, staring ahead of him, frowning heavily.

Old Hobard came hobbling up, and threw himself flat on his face, hammering his fists on the ground, invoking the earth and calling her name.

'Molm, Malma, Malmanna, Mah!' he cried. 'Do not cast us away! Mah! Mah! Malmanna! We are your children. We have lived here for seven years. We have used fire and cleared the land with caution. We have honoured you here for seven years. Our hoes and ploughs have not wounded you more than flea bites. We have praised you with dance and song, in the winter, too, when you slept, so that you should have good dreams. But the trolls are breaking you, Malmanna, tearing you to pieces. They're stamping on you . . .'

'Shut your mouth, man,' said Halva, on her way past him. 'How do you know she likes us any better than them. They're her children, too, and they've lived here longer than we have.'

'Salt,' said old Hobard, not listening to her, but suddenly remembering something else. 'Show me where you met them, the trolls,' he went on to the children. 'If we can find their footsteps, then we can get the better of them. We'll drop red-hot ashes and salt where they've trodden.'

King Tulle had finished thinking now. He took

Kotkel's horn from him and blew hard on it, sounding the note that meant everyone should at once come to the space in front of the hall.

And when they had all crowded round him, he told them that everyone should flee to the islands, not to Rummel Island, but to the next one. They should pack what they had of food, tools and equipment, carrying all of it down to the boats on the shore.

'You and you and you,' he said, naming several men, 'can start ferrying over the goats and children to start with, and the older ones can look after the younger ones.'

They were to equip themselves as if for an army camp, he said, and given time, perhaps they could wage war against the trolls in some way, but at this moment it was first and foremost a question of escaping with their lives.

There was such a hurry that no one really had time to worry about their fears, though it was as if there were an icy breeze at the back of their necks and their gaze kept being drawn to the forest. Old Hobard went about mumbling: 'Woe is me, was I wrong after all? Is he doomed, and all of us with him? But the Star of Victory was the one burning over the great sea that year he was born.' His jaw wagged so much that he slurred and slobbered his words and annoyed everyone who heard him.

Towards the evening, Tulaborg grew empty and silent. All the people had rowed and sailed and paddled and poled their way across the sound.

Practically everything loose had been taken over as well. But King Tulle himself strode round the hill, to see that no one was left behind, he said to himself, but the truth was that he probably found it difficult to tear himself away. The sun was glowing in the north-west, just beginning to sink.

He stood on the patch in front of the hall with its bold dragon heads. Inside it was already dark. He went up to the throne, touching each upright on the way. He took down his bark-crown and pressed it firmly down on his head. Then he sat down on the throne, running his hands over its carvings, and he was so tired that it felt as if he would never ever be able to rise again.

But a moment later, he did so all the same because he had heard a noise outside, the unexpected sound of someone humming. The sun had gone now and mists were rising from the marshy meadows round the river-mouth. The forest was black. And there was a light in the bakery.

Halva was in there, baking bread.

King Tulle stood in the doorway, hardly able to believe his eyes, but at the same time he was not at all surprised. Perhaps he was too tired, and Halva had always been one to do unexpected things.

He had hardly seen her for several years. Just as she had in Sigga Valley, she lived by herself in a turf hut. People called for her when they needed help, when a child was to be born, or some cloth was to be dyed, or when someone was afflicted with fever.

An oven of clay and stones had been built above the hearth in the middle of the bakery floor, and Halva was pushing sour-bread loaves into it to bake. She looked up at Tulle in the doorway, then stopped humming and smiled.

'Do you want a taste?' she said.

Tulle replied sharply: 'Stop that, now. Run down to the shore and take my rowing-boat. There's still time to get away.'

'Now, steady, steady,' she said. 'The bread will burn.'

He thought perhaps she had become confused with age and fright, and he tried to talk some sense into her. 'Off you go now,' he said. 'What do a few loaves matter when it comes to your life?'

Quite calmly, she took out the baked loaves and pushed in the unbaked ones, and they smelt so good that his mouth watered. 'You can't live without bread,' she said. 'You know that. That's the very last of the flour, and now we'll have to wait for the new rye, if we don't want to have to make do with ground roots and bark.'

Suddenly Tulle grew angry. Taking a great stride inside, he lifted up the little old woman and carried her out under his arm like a pig, running with her down the hillside to the shore. At first she struggled. But he plumped her down into his little rowing-boat and pushed it out from the shore. 'Row now,' he panted, 'and I'll finish the baking.'

'You can't do that, King Tulle,' she said. 'And

how are you going to get away yourself, if you give your boat to me?' In a twinkling, she had turned it, jumped ashore, nipped under his outstetched arms and trotted on up the hill. She was so small, she was scarcely visible, her grey dress blending in with the dusk. But when she turned her head, her eyes were glowing like translucent fires.

'Now it's just like the beginning, King Tulle,' she cried over her shoulder, laughing at him. 'No one but you and me here on the hill, and your enemies on the way.'

Then he thought it must be true, what people said, that she was only half human, and that she was doing this to welcome her friends the trolls. And he felt downhearted and hopeless in spirit, his feet dragging behind him, so he had to stop and lean against a tree.

For now they were coming, the trolls, roaring like thunder, strong winds swirling round them in the air. They raised their feet high, and came sniffing the air and stretching out their necks. One of them caught sight of Tulle, and letting out a loud 'Ho Ho' he looked round for something to throw. But there was neither stone nor branch handy, so the troll took an armlet off and threw that. Tulle felt the armlet glance by his head, and he saw the troll black out the whole sky.

Then he heard Halva calling. It was remarkable what a strong rich voice she had, although she herself was so small. She was using words that King Tulle only half understood.

'Archaeans of the forest!' she cried. 'I am offering you the strength of man, the strength of fire and the strength of earth in these small loaves. I am offering power and glory to whoever can bear it.'

They stopped. She threw the loaves up to them. They caught them and turned them over in their hands. They sniffed at them, grunting and grousing to each other. Then one of the trolls began to eat, liking the taste, and all of them immediately greedily gobbled up what they had been given.

Halva was standing right in amongst them, barely reaching up to their knees. As soon as one had finished his loaf, she threw up another. This went on for quite a while, until one of the trolls began to groan.

'Claws tearing at my belly . . .'

'That's the strength taking hold,' said Halva.

'Ravaging and tearing and tormenting . . .'

'That's the strength glowing and filling you. Soon you'll have had enough.'

The trolls bent double and began to roar. They raised their feet to trample on Halva, but she hastily slid away from them. They bumped into each other and one sat down on the roof of the bakery, which collapsed. 'Water!' howled another of them, and they staggered northwards towards the meadows, where the river ran out into the sea. Then they died of their stomach-pains, there on the meadows, and they all turned to stone. Now it was dawn.

Halva stood beside Tulle. She was very tired, and between her yawns, she said: 'That's settled that, then.

Now you can get the people back home again.'

'Did you put poison in the bread?' said Tulle.

'No, there was no need. The rye draws strength from the earth, and is baked in fire. As I told you, strength of earth, strength of fire. And then there was the sour-dough. It outrages a stomach not used to it. And fresh from the oven, too. No doubt you've had a stomach-ache in your day. I know that, me who looked after you as a child and gave you brews to drink.'

'I'd have preferred to have thrust them through with spear or sword,' said King Tulle.

To that she just shrugged her shoulders and snorted. Then she trotted off, but stopped after a few steps.

'Come here, King Tulle,' she said. 'And see what the trolls have left behind.'

It was the armlet that had been thrown and had glanced by Tulle's head. Everything else the trolls had worn or had with them had turned to stone, all except the armlet that had been thrown before they died. It was made of copper mixed with gold, with decorations all round the edge.

'That's a much more handsome crown than your old one,' she said.

Tulle took off his crown of bark and tried the gold armlet on his head instead. 'It's heavy,' he said. 'It rubs.'

'The greater the kingdom, the heavier the crown,' said Halva. 'You've inherited forest lands from the trolls now.'

She trotted off. She was very tired. So was King Tulle. He went to bed and slept for half a day before he had the energy to row over to the island to bring his people back.

The island on which they had sought protection later came to be called Troll Island, though no trolls went there until many hundreds of years later. That first happened when the land had risen so much that you could walk there on dry ground. And the trolls that went there were mostly only small ones. The larger ones had been forced away as the number of people increased. They had either died or disappeared to the east and the north. It should be noted that they were not at all the foolish clumsy dunderheads the sagas of later times made them out to be. They were forest creatures, lithe and strong and beautiful in their own way. But they thought differently from people, so in the end they came off worst.

# 3
# HE MARRIES

The people of Tulle thrived, clearing the forest and spreading out eastwards along the coast. So many children were born that although half of them died during the winters, there was nevertheless a constant chatter of children's voices everywhere. But King Tulle himself gradually became more and more morose.

One day in high summer, he was in such low spirits that he could not find the strength to see a single person. He took a boat and rowed away. The weather was good, truly fine and warm, but he sat heavily shrouded in a haze of indifference and weariness. It seemed to him that all the sorrows and difficulties of his life had simultaneously agreed to meet and gather round him. The worst of it was that he had no one to wake him up and comfort him when he had nightmares. For it still happened that he dreamt about Sote and Laff sometimes, seeing them coming, climbing in over the fence. And he dreamt about his mother. She had vanished, perhaps even died, in his early childhood. Sometimes he also dreamt that he was leading his people on a journey through dangerous country, all of them huddling behind him, holding on to his cloak, and the weight of their hands gradually became so great that he stumbled, thinking he would suffocate.

He went ashore to the west of the rivermouth, hauling the boat on land and tying it up. Then he sloped off towards the forest, his shoulders drooping and his steps heavy.

After he had been walking for a while, he met an old man who said to him: 'You look poorly, King Tulle.'

Tulle frowned. The old man was a stranger, thin and lank and as grey as lichen, barefooted and wearing skins. 'Who are you?' said Tulle, but the old man laughed instead of answering, and said:

'Yes indeed, you're no doubt a handsome man, but clouded and lonely.'

King Tulle grunted.

'I would like to propose to you on my daughter's behalf,' said the old man. 'She's beautiful and well-disposed, and she has all the coastland from here to Urnas in the west to bring with her. I'll tell you how things are. Her mother is dead and I'm an old man now. Before I go off away into the forest, I wish to see her settled. Would you like to come with me to see her, King Tulle?'

Tulle had no desire to, but he went all the same.

They walked westwards along the shore for a while

until they came to a bay. On the far side of the bay there were some limes, great trees with branches bending in all directions, the lowest scraping the ground, and they were in flower. The clusters of flowers were hanging so thickly between the leaves that the trees seemed to be clad in honey-fur, and filled with the hum of every kind of flying creature. And the scent was strong. King Tulle stood with his head back, gazing up at the tree. He had never seen anything so beautiful before.

'Libite, Vidiranga, Hassa-Unn!' called the old man.

There was a rustling in the leaves and two hands appeared, then a face and then the whole girl. She looked like none of the daughters of Tulle's people, but was very slim and dark. Her eyes were slanting and dark-brown, her nose long, making her look almost like a fox. Her hair came down to her knees and her dress of thin soft leather hid her feet. As she walked towards King Tulle to greet him, he saw that she was lame.

'I'll tell you how things are,' said the old man. 'One of her feet has been smaller than the other since birth, which is why no one on our side of the water will have her.'

The girl bowed and Tulle placed his hands on his chest and bowed back. He found it difficult to take his eyes off her. She moved softly and gracefully, so that her limp seemed almost like a dance. He took her by the hand.

'She's capable and clever and gentle, as long as you don't annoy her,' said the old man. 'Sit down here on the grass and rest for a while, King Tulle, and think the matter over.'

Tulle already felt friendly towards the girl, and she also looked gently at him with her unusual eyes. He felt sweet and warm all over, as if light flames of honey had leapt inside his skin. But he did not know what to say to her. He sat down on the grass and she sat down beside him, but the old man remained standing, looking down at them both. Tulle wished that he would at least turn his back on them for a while, but he did not.

'Do you want her?' said the old man.

Tulle nodded.

'In exchange,' said the old man, 'I ask you to promise that you will always respect her and keep her well.'

Tulle promised. They agreed that the wedding should be held in Tulaborg in three days' time.

'Now I will show you the boundaries of my kingdom.'

He put on a floppy fur hat, took a stave in his hand and began to walk westwards along the shore. Tulle was forced to follow, although he would have preferred to stay with the girl. He had still not heard her voice.

He and the old man came to a headland of sand and stones, where dry spicy herbs grew, and there were two thick pines growing alongside each other, but leaning in different directions. Like a fence round the two trees were a number of twisted and deformed small pines. The old man walked in below them, bowed and sang out a long verse. 'Now, King Tulle,' he said. 'I've told those that rule here that you are their new lord and master. Take your knife, make a cut in your left middle finger and let three drops of blood fall here between the trees. Then they'll always recognize you.'

Tulle did so, but the drops were more than three, as he cut himself unnecessarily deeply.

Beyond the pines lay a heap of stones, with skulls of elk and other animals lying in a circle round them.

The headland was the first boundary marker. They went to several more; a little island they waded out to, a cove round and dark like a pot, and each time the old man stopped and sang, letting Tulle leave his drop of blood. Then they came to a stream that was the boundary to the west, and they followed it upstream. All the time, Tulle had to take sights, learning the land by heart, the old man said. Here and there, they came upon flowering limes, and each time Tulle smelt the scent, he drew in a deep breath. The old man noticed and smiled to himself.

Towards evening, they came to the foot of a mountain. The old man told Tulle to pick up as large a boulder as he could manage, then carry it right up to to the peak without stopping to rest on the way. Tulle chose a boulder and began walking up the mountainside with it, but he was wearier than he had reckoned with, and the mountain was steep, higher than any other in the district. He walked more and more slowly, breathing more and more heavily, but he forced himself to go on and not give up, and thus he arrived at the very top. There was nothing growing there and he could see for miles and miles. To the south lay the sea and to the north the great forests. The sun was just going down, round and a soft dull red. The whole world, except the sun, was blue.

At the very top of the mountain was a heap of stones, and beside it, the old man was standing waiting, his finger in his mouth. He gestured to Tulle to place his stone on the heap. Nearby was a crevice, narrow and very deep. The old man went down on his knees and thrust his head into the crevice, calling and bellowing down there so that it went on echoing a long time afterwards.

Then Tulle had to drop blood down into the crevice as well, feeling uneasy as he did so, but at the same time, he was so tired that he did not really mind about anything, as weary as he had been on the day he had killed Sote and Laff.

When they came down to the forest again, Tulle said:

'Who lives there?'

The old man shook his head and flailed about with his arms. 'Someone. I don't know. Perhaps he has no name. Powerful, he is, though. Fights with a stone axe.'

'A troll?'

'No, not a troll.'

They made camp for the night and Tulle lit a fire. He had left home without food, but the old man had strips of dried meat in his tunic pouch, and there were bilberries with which to wet their mouths.

The next morning, they followed the northern boundary of the kingdom as far as the river, where they parted and Tulle went home. He arrived back in Tulaborg at about dinner time, covered with sweat, and without washing or eating or drinking anything or speaking to anyone, he went straight up to the hall. He took the great horn and blew the assembly note for his people. He told them he was going to marry in two days' time. He said he wanted the wedding arranged as grandly as possible. But he refused to answer any questions.

Hobard and others with him had for many years kept on telling Tulle that he ought to get married. But now that he had fulfilled their wishes, they were still not content. They said he was careless and foolish and had gone against ancient custom. They followed him down the hill to have it all said at least to his back.

But when he got away from them into his bedchamber, Halva was standing there waiting with a bowl of milk, and while he drank it, she sniffed the air round him. 'What are you sniffing at?' he said.

'You mind your own business, and I'll mind mine,' she said, with a smile.

Once Tulle's people had had their say and overcome their disappointment that he was not going to marry anyone of his own kind, they eagerly set about the wedding preparations, everyone trying to outdo the other with ideas and industry.

Tulle could hardly sleep for the remaining nights. His head was humming and singing, beautiful dark leaves and honey-pale clusters of flowers danced before his eyes. As he walked about, he kept smiling to himself. He joined in the selecting of the bridal trees, but took no part in the customary fun between the young men who were to carry them back, and the young girls who tried to hinder their progress. He thought that as his bride liked limes, he would plant saplings all round the hall, but Halva said it was the wrong time of year to move young trees and he would have to wait until the autumn. But he decided that the bedchamber should be decorated with flowering lime, mayweed and bedstraw – nothing but yellow and white flowers, like honey and milk and sun. He sank clay pots with water inside them into the little hearth in the middle of the floor of the chamber. The flowers were placed there, and he spent a long time arranging them so that they would look beautiful and as if they were growing out of the floor.

Neither did he waste much time on eating, waving aside porridge and meat because it fastened in his throat. But Halva brought her bowls, fresh milk and sour milk, egg whipped with honey and stewed soft fruits.

In good time on the wedding day, King Tulle took the long-boat, decorated with foliage and flowers and quilts on all the seats, and was rowed to the meeting-place the old man had agreed on. This was below Rivermouth Mountain on the other side of the rivermouth, where there were long green meadows between the forest and the water. He stood waiting on the shore in his best summer clothes of bleached linen, embroidered in red and blue and brown round all the hems. He wore a blue cloak, leather shoes with tassels on them on his feet, and the troll-crown on his head. His men stood in two groups, all with spears in their hands and bright pennants fastened below the spearheads, Kotkel and Egil at their head.

Libite came out of the forest, swaying across the meadow on a litter of foliage. She was seated on a leafy throne, the leaves singing in the wind, a wreath of lime flowers on her head, and she was wearing a very long wide gown made of the blossom and leaves of the lime tree.

Her father was walking beside her, his floppy fur hat in his hand, and he also had a lime-wreath on his grizzled head. He was leaning on his stave.

The swaying leafy litter stopped and King Tulle lifted down his bride. He caught sight of brown furry legs beneath the hanging greenery, and he also heard small panting gasps, but the bearers did not show themselves, and King Tulle was far too excited and eager to bother about that. He carried the girl into the boat, and she bowed in farewell to her father, who did not wish to come with them across the water. He remained on the shore until they had all stepped ashore on the Tulaborg side, then he took off his wreath and threw it into the sea. Then pressing his hat down on his head, he walked across the meadows towards the forest, and from beneath the leafy throne, eight slim reddish-brown creatures ran out and followed him. No one ever saw him again.

The wedding celebrations were divided into different parts: first came the formal part. King Tulle lifted his bride ashore, and preceded by pipers and fiddlers, and followed by all the people in their best clothes, wreaths on their heads and branches in their hands, they walked in procession up to the shrine. There they bowed to the invisible presences, made offerings to the spring and drank its waters – he out of her hand and she out of his. Hobard kept mumbling to himself and looking self-important, wishing he could have conducted a really grand and lengthy and lavish service with sacrifices of different kinds, but as Tulle would not allow him to, he had to be content with mumbling. But he had convinced himself that his mumbling was the foundation on which the whole wedding and marriage rested.

Then came the banquet. They had put up trestle tables outside the hall and built a leafy bower for the couple to sit inside. Everything the people had been able to find in the way of food and drink had been placed there, from legs of dried meat to freshly picked berries. There was milk and mead, ale and water, boiled and grilled fish, bread and cakes, and porridge and cream.

Neither Tulle nor his bride ate very much, but they had to stay seated at the table until everyone else had eaten their fill. She sat so still that he wondered if she were frightened or sorrowful and homesick. But he could not ask her, as there was such a noise going on all round them.

Then came the fun. The tables were taken away and the dancing began. Tulle led his bride out by the hand and the fiddlers tuned up. But just as they were about to start, he wondered whether she would know what to do. So he bent over her and said: 'You needn't, if you don't want to.' She gave his hand a little squeeze in reply, and then began to dance. And true enough, she moved in a completely individual way, like a bird or a forest creature. She kept time and Tulle, leaping and kicking beside her, her hand in his, felt clumsy, again and again going wrong, because he kept looking at her instead of thinking about the steps.

After the bridal dance, there were other dances, the old women's dance and the old men's, the warriors' dance, which was nothing much more than stamping on the spot, hands on each other's shoulders, and then the young people's dance, and long swerving running-sets, ring-dances and chain-dances in which everyone joined in. The pipers blew until they were red in the face, the drums thumped, old Hobard plucked away on his home-made string instrument that he maintained was a harp.

Then there were the children, hordes of children, who made as much noise as they could with bits of wood and pots covered with parchment and ordinary stems of grass between their thumbs. And the people sang.

At sunset, bonfires were lit on the river meadows and the people danced in and out between the fires. This was to go on all night. But then Halva came along with several other old women and carried the bride back with them to the sleeping chamber where she and Tulle were going to live.

Tulle had to leap over fires and drink in thanks to the people in mead before he was allowed to go after her.

He walked alone through the dark hall, which was empty and chilly, as no one lived there in summer. He hung his crown up on the throne, then went into the chamber.

Two wax candles were burning in the hearth on the floor. A faint light was coming through the little window and the girl was sitting on the bench in front of the great cupboard bed, waiting for him.

Her leafy gown had withered and curled at the hem, so now Tulle could see her bare feet. The left one was a fox's foot, a tiny, furry paw.

At first he thought he was seeing things, as he was dizzy and confused from all the mead he had drunk and the heady scent of limes.

Then it seemed as if those flames of honey that had leapt and played inside him had grown too great, stinging and burning him more and more. The whole room seemed to be on fire. He had been cheated. His bride was not a woman, but some kind of troll.

'This is the revenge of the trolls,' he thought. 'They're regaining power of the land. Our children will be half-trolls.'

At the same time, he had to admit that the old man, her father, had in some way told him the truth. And as he had promised to respect her and keep her well always, his honour and destiny were bound to hers, whatever he chose to do.

He thought about how people, his brothers far away in Sigga Valley in particular, would laugh if he broke his marriage vows and forsook her. And he thought that, after all, the girls, ordinary girls that he had seen and known, all looked like turnips in comparison with her. He also thought that even if any of them would want to have him after this, then he could not even contemplate celebrating another wedding.

Then he thought about those lonely nights when it had seemed as if hands of darkness were weaving bands round his heart and jerking them tight every time he was about to fall asleep.

The fire in him died down, and he could see again and breathe again without it hurting. His bride had sat quite still all that time, looking at him with her slanting eyes.

Then his last thought was that she, too, was lonely.

'I hope you will be content here with me,' said King Tulle. 'Though it'll probably be different from what you're used to.'

'I think we'll both be content,' she replied.

That was the first time he had heard her voice. It was low and slightly husky, but resonant. It was a voice that later he never grew tired of. She could sing, but she could also howl like a fox. She could change haven and transform herself completely into a fox if she wished to. When enemies approached, she slipped unnoticed out to observe. When winters were hard and their needs great, she kept the whole of Tulle's household alive by going out hunting beneath the snow and digging out forest mice.

# 4

# HE IS GIVEN STRIKER THE SWORD

During the summer, Tulle's household lived in shelters and huts round about. But when the cold time of year began, they all moved back into the hall. There were several beds built between the uprights and the walls, some as large as rooms, with roofs and walls and hatches to close. Farthest down, to the left of the door, they did the cooking and to the right they kept their tools, and from there ran a turf-covered passage leading to the cattle-shed.

Kotkel, who had been herdsman as a child and had been chased by the trolls, had married and had been given a farm of his own a short way up the river. He and his wife had invited Tulle to their place for the baptismal feast for their first son, and Tulle had gone with Egil and a few of his men. His wife had stayed at home, as she was expecting their fourth child and was less mobile than usual.

It was autumn, a day of storm and rain and early darkness. King Tulle was expected home, but was late. Evening came with no news of him. Queen Libite sat at the top of the hall sewing on a hide. She did not like wool, neither as clothing nor to handle. Too rough, she said, so she kept to skins or linen. Beside her, Halva and several other women were sitting spinning. The men were making things. One was carving fish-hooks out of bone, another patching his seal-skin slippers, some carving wood and flinging the shavings on to the fire. They did not have a fire the whole length of the hearth, but only at the upper part, where they were all huddled round. Because of the weather, they could not have the roof-hatch open, so the smoke collected round the spurs, as if clouds had come indoors.

Queen Libite was worried, time and time again raising her head and listening, and every time she did so, the dogs whined and crept closer to the fire. When the others asked what the matter was, she just shook her head. She asked Hulda, who saw to the their meals, to put out a jar of ale to warm. Hulda had also married, and there were several children playing on the dry rushes on the floor.

Hobard was telling stories. He did so at every possible opportunity. He was very long-winded and extended everything he said by repeating himself.

It was hard to hurry him, and even harder to interrupt him, especially when he was relating about the time he had ended his loyalty to King Steinhulf and King Bork, and had instead chosen to serve King Tulle. He had fought his way through to Tuntula! Enemy heads had fallen like fir-cones in a storm! And at the last moment he had reached Tulaborg and come to the aid of King Tulle, who had then lived alone . . . well, alone . . . King Tulle had lived there with eleven beautiful women who were hairy from nose to ankle . . .

'Don't forget they had horns and beards and tails, too,' said Halva.

Before Hobard had time to answer, a thumping sound came from up on the roof, the timbers creaking and groaning, the supports swaying under the strain. Queen Libite flew up from her place and stood there, quite tense. The dogs' hackles rose and they trembled and bared their fangs. The women shrieked, all except Halva, and the men scuttled round for their weapons.

'Was it a tree falling on to the house?'

'Is it the trolls?'

'Is it the enemy?'

Queen Libite spoke to Hulda. 'Hold the dogs,' she said, and then she glided quickly away, past the throne and into the bedchamber. Quite soon after her marriage, she had dug a secret passage from under the bed, down under the earth, leading to several openings out among the pine trees. Only Tulle and Halva and she herself knew about it. Now she turned herself into a fox and slipped out through it. She looked round in the rain and the dark, then returned, her hair wet, and she told the people what she had seen.

'It's the Iron-Forest Bird sitting on the roof.'

'The Iron-Forest Bird?'

Hobard had heard of it and began to whimper. The Iron-Forest was in the north or the east, inhabited by

evil forces and beasts that destroyed people. The Iron-Forest Bird was as big as a horse, its wingspan four times the length of a man, its feathers as hard as swords, all of them, its claws like the curved sabres of the Orient, its eyes of fire, its beak . . . its beak . . . its beak was Death itself.

'He's eaten King Tulle!' squealed Hulda loudly. And then the children also began to cry, the dogs whined and the men wanted to rush out and fight. Queen Libite ordered them all to be still.

'Whoever goes out will be devoured,' she said. 'Like when the woodpecker takes a bark-worm. If King Tulle is still alive, he's on his way home, and in far greater danger for every step he takes. We must kill the bird before he comes within its reach.'

She told Hulda to keep the children quiet where they were. The dogs were firmly tied up. The fire was moved nearer to the door, torches were lit and put into their iron holders. She divided the men into two groups, placing them on each side of the door and giving them a long stool to hold between them. The stool was made of a split log with inserted legs. They held it up by its legs. Queen Libite took the three best spears they had in the hall, bound them firmly together with a strap, and then opened the door. It opened inwards, and she pulled it right back against the wall.

During their preparations, the bird had remained quite still on the roof all the time, just as great birds of prey sit still, turning only their heads. Now, as the door creaked on its hardwood tenons and the firelight shone out on to the slope outside, it rose with a roaring rush of its great wings. The animals in the cattle-shed bleated and bellowed, tearing at their bindings, so Halva hurried through the passage to see that they did not injure themselves. At a sign from Libite, the men raised the stool high above the door-post, their arms stretched up straight. The bird hovered flapping in the air by the gable of the hall, the draught from its wings so ferocious that they could neither hear anything else nor hardly think. Libite, the bound spears in her hand, walked halfway out through the doorway.

Immediately, she flung herself back inside again, with one great leap backwards and to one side. This all happened so quickly that the men saw nothing but a blur. The Iron-Forest Bird had hurtled down, snapping at her, its beak-halves slashing like swords. It thrust its head in through the doorway.

'Now!' cried Libite, so loudly and shrilly that they heard her above the noise.

The men crashed the long stool down over the Iron-Forest Bird's neck, then hurled themselves down on to it with all their weight. Then Libite thrust the three-headed spear into the eye that the bird had turned towards her, with such strength that the spear came out of the other eye. The Iron-Forest Bird let out a terrible scream, then died, blood and mess running all over the floor. Halva came with an armful of dry reeds that she flung down on to the pool.

The storm and rain came pouring through the doorway. The torches went out, the flames extinguished by the draught, the smoke swirling round them so that it was difficult to see. Coughing, Queen Libite began pulling out the bird's feathers. They were hard and rattled against each other. Panting a little, she said: 'We must pluck it in a strip across its crop and belly, then we can cut it open and see if it has eaten anyone . . .'

But before they had time to do anything else, they heard cries and calls from outside and saw the faint glint of horn-lamps. It was King Tulle, unhurt, approaching with his party.

That night they let the Iron-Forest Bird lie where it was, only dragging it away sufficiently so that they could get past and get the door closed. But the next day, everyone in the neighbourhood gathered round to look and feel and wonder and talk and shiver with delight.

Queen Libite was with them. She took no part in the chatter and talk, but she had a stone in her hand with which she struck the claws and beak of the Iron-Forest Bird. She asked Tulle and Egil for help in freeing the beak from the skull and the claws from the feet. It was heavy work and they had to use stones for it, because the whole bird, except its eyes, was as hard as iron.

The work went best with an old flint-saw Hobard had brought with him from Sigga Valley. At first he did not want to lend it, complaining that it was sacred, as it had once fallen from heaven as a gift of Tindera. But Libite just looked at him; she had power in her eyes if she wanted to use it, and then he gave in.

They dragged the corpse of the bird to the marsh between the hills north-east of Tulaborg. The highest of them, from where King Tulle had seen his land for the very first time, was called Green Heights. Below Green Heights was an open swamp. They sank the Iron-Forest Bird into that, after first cutting it open and filling it with stones. Hobard stood on a hummock and babbled away over it with his arms outstretched and his hair standing on end in the wind.

Queen Libite put the Iron-Forest Bird's beak and claws into a sack. Then she put on her great leather cloak, slung the sack on her back and said to King Tulle that she had something to do out in the forest. She would be away for three or four days, she said.

He did not want to let her go, reminding her that she was expecting their child, and she had not wanted to go with him to Kottrodjan, Kotkel's farm. She had already exposed herself to enough danger, he said, holding her tight in his arms.

She replied that her errand was important, and that she had eight brothers in the forest who would protect her. He had never before heard that she had any brothers, and was astonished, asking her to tell him more. But before the words were out of his mouth, she had in some way made herself so small and slim that she had slipped out of his arms and was on her way to the forest.

On the fourth day, she returned with a sword in her

sack. It shone blue when she lifted it and it had grooves for blood and symbols engraved along the blade. The handle was black. The whole had been forged from the beak and claws of the Iron-Forest Bird, she explained. A relative of hers who was a smith had done it. She handed it to Tulle, saying that now it was his and it would bring good fortune in battle to him, and now he had to find a name for it.

He had been so uneasy during her absence and was so pleased to see her back again and was so full of questions that he could not find any better name than Striker.

# 5
# HIS BROTHER COMES

Some time after King Tulle had been given the sword, his brother Bork came riding with an escort of twenty-seven men. The ground trembled beneath the horses' hoofs, and the thunder of them could be heard long before they hove into sight.

Bork was quite tall and handsome, but he was fat. His face was pale, his hair and beard dark, and he had shaped his moustache so that it formed a bow round his mouth. He was richly clothed, his red cloak covering the whole of his horse's hindquarters when he was riding and reaching right down to his ankles when he was standing on the ground. He wore spurs.

Tulle received him outside the hall. Bork said that he had come visiting to show that he bore no ill-will towards Tulle, who had so unkindly weakened the family by leaving Sigga Valley and inadvisedly marrying out of the forest. He had brought gifts with him, he said. A packhorse was led forward and Tulle was pleased, thinking he was to be given the horse – they had no horses at all in Tuntula at the time. But Bork's men loosened the thongs round a hide wrapped round a pack of cloth, and it was the cloth that was the gift. It was foreign cloth, with gold threads in it, and Bork praised it a great deal, almost as if he were a merchant. The other gift was an iron shield, rather small and battered. It had belonged to their father, old King Sigulf of Sigga Valley. Bork boasted about that too. It had been in many honourable battles, he said, and it might also still prove useful, although it was scratched and slightly rusty round the edges.

Libite then came out to welcome him with a horn of ale. Without a word, she handed the horn to Bork with a bow. She was not pleased. As always when strangers came, she was wearing shoes. Their own people, indeed all the people of Tuntula, knew that she was half a fox, but they pretended not to. At first, they had been a trifle afraid of her as well as of her relatives in the forest, and they had also been uneasy lest Tulle's and her children should have tails. But now that she had given birth to three perfectly ordinary, well-formed children, and was once again large with child, her subjects were all proud of her, even worshipful.

Tulle had space made for the horses in the cattle-shed and Bork was given the best bed in the hall. His men were packed into the others and filled nearly all of them, so Tulle's own men had to sleep on benches and on the floor. Egil made himself a sleeping-place by the door of the chamber. He felt uneasy at having so many strangers in the house, and wanted to sleep where he could warn Tulle if anything happened at night.

Hobard had similar fears. Together, they bored a hole through the wall of the chamber, pulling a thong through the hole and fastening it to a piece of wood that they balanced on a ledge inside the chamber. If anything should happen, they explained, Egil would pull the thong and the piece of wood would fall – then Tulle would have been warned without anyone knowing.

Only Tulle and Libite and their children slept inside the chamber. It was one of Libite's peculiarities that she did not like sleeping in the company of others. Bork did not say how long he intended to stay.

In the evening, when the men took off their outer clothing to go to bed, it was evident that they had recent injuries. Tulle said that he had an excellent healing-woman in his household, and he called for Halva to see to the men. Bork said that was quite unnecessary. They had only been in a little skirmish, nothing to worry about – and he flung himself down on the bed, belching loudly and demanding ale.

But while Halva and Hulda washed and tended the men's injuries, they heard the real reason for Bork's visit, which was that he had lost in battle against his brother, King Steinhulf, and had been driven out of Sigga Valley.

Bork was an unpleasant and tiresome guest, and he soon began to smell. He and his men ate and drank far too much, and their many long legs took up space in the hall. Their horses all too soon put an end to the fodder, and it was so late in the year that the grass was dead and there was nothing to collect but moss and heather.

King Tulle drove Bork and his men out to hunt, or at least to play ball – they did no ordinary work. In that way, he managed to get the hall aired occasionally and some additions to the food supplies. Only the most severely injured men remained sitting by the fire.

Among them was one who had injured his shoulder. He was a foreigner from one of the Blue Countries in the south, and his name, or the beginning of it, was something like Binnab. He was thin and large-nosed, brown and black. He spoke hesitantly, but the children, who liked him, understood him very well all the same. He liked telling stories to them, long ones that might last for days, and short ones he called tales. He told them about the southern deserts where there was gold. 'What's a desert?' said the children. He explained – sand. He had been riding there on a camel. 'What's a camel?' – An animal higher than an elk, with an even larger hump, and smaller ears and no horns, with a face more like a goat. He had come to an oasis . . . 'What's an oasis?' . . . an oasis where there were steps leading down into the sand to the city of the ancient kings. They were all buried there, deep down in the sand, with wreaths of ears of wheat and celeriac round their necks. And there were bird-women in the air. He had met one with great wings and she had dived at him like an eagle. He had fought her for a long time and had won in the end and they had become friends, and she had given him a weapon, the like of which did not exist in all the Blue Countries: a spear made of the longest feather from her right wing.

When he came to the end of the story, he smiled at the children round him on the dry reeds on the floor. 'Things like that don't happen here,' he said.

King Tulle's elder son's name was Tile.

'Yes,' he said. 'Something almost like that happened here. Father's sword is made from the beak and claws of a great bird, and it's better than anyone anyone else's sword.'

'No, is it?' said Binnab.

'Yes,' said all the children, and they *all* started telling him about the evening when the Iron-Forest Bird came down on the roof. They ran hither and thither all over the hall, showing him what had happened, and the smallest children, scarcely able to talk yet, grew more and more wide-eyed, stammering: 'Bird – bird,' and ran round flapping their arms. When they showed him how the bird had died, they lay down on the floor together and twisted their necks and wiggled their arms. Binnab laughed at them. They were so noisy that the other men, sitting with their ale over at the games boards, also looked up and paid attention.

Then Binnab told them more stories.

One day, Bork asked King Tulle to accompany him on an otter hunt. His men had seen otter tracks by one of the streams that ran into the river. They had also found the otter's holt and were setting about damming the stream and flooding the holt.

The weather was still and grey, thin snow covering the ground, but the water had not yet frozen over. When Tulle left, Libite came out with him and stood on the hillside, watching him go.

Tulle had left Egil at home to see to the work on the land and took with him a young man called Kare. Bork had his attendant Sigge with him. The rest of the men were up at the otter stream. All four of them got into the boat, and Kare and Sigge took the oars. Halfway across to the Rivermouth Mountain shore, Bork began complaining.

'Your thrales are insolent,' he said. 'I wanted an otter net yesterday, and they said there wasn't one. I said I wanted one made by today, and they insolently replied that they had no time. I beat them of course. It seems to me that they need a bit of softening up. You should have them properly flogged and cut the heel tendons of at least a few.'

'I have no thrales,' said Tulle.

Bork snorted, pulling his red cloak round him and thinking that he certainly had come very far out into the wilds.

Tulle said that he and his people had plenty to do without delving into each other's origins, so he had very early on decided that all men in Tuntula would be regarded as free. For some of the newcomers, this had been difficult to get used to at first, but now they all liked things as they were.

Bork said softly that now he understood. 'Cleverly

calculated, that was,' he said. 'It'd be difficult for you to keep order between thrales and freemen according to ancient custom, when your own mother was a thrale, born in the ashes . . .'

Tulle did not know much about his mother, only that she had been captured and taken to Sigga Valley from some distant country. It was not easy for him to reply. He clenched his fists and said nothing as the boat glided on, leaving long shiny ripples on the water. As they turned towards the shore beneath Rivermouth Mountain, he said: '*I* think that the least of our guilts here on earth is that we allow ourselves to be born. More degrading deeds come later, to each and every one of us. The most degrading is to degrade others.'

Bork laughed. 'Let yourself be eaten alive by lice, then I'll believe you, pretty talker!' And he stepped ashore.

Up on Tulaborg hill, Libite stood watching the red cloak swelling out against the white snow and the black alder woods and the green pine forest higher up. She watched Tulle's dark-blue cloak go ashore, and the two other men, grey and brown, haul up the boat.

'Now I've seen your kingdom,' said Bork. 'It's not at all bad, and could be better if it were looked after. I would like to offer you my assistance. I would stay here as joint ruler, provided you build me decent houses and a hall similar to your own.'

Tulle replied that he did not wish for any such assistance.

'You are unfriendly towards me,' said Bork. 'And you do not deal wisely. Remember that it was I who persuaded Steinhulf to give you the twelve goats you demanded from your mother, although, of course, as a captured thrale, she had no right to property. I was the one to lay the foundations of your well-being. It would be reasonable now that you gave me half your lands.'

Tulle replied that he did not think that was in any way reasonable.

'Then I challenge you here and now – I shall have your kingdom, half or all of it!' Bork had grown angry and red in the face.

Tulle replied that he did not wish to fight. 'For you are my brother. And my sword is better than yours.'

'We are only half-brothers, and as far as the sword is concerned, I'd gladly exchange them!' said Bork, with a loud laugh.

He drew his sword and began to slash out at Tulle, who retreated nimbly, fending off the blows with Striker, but without striking back.

Up on Tulaborg hill, Libite stood watching the red cloak and the dark-blue cloak circling and swirling round each other. She called to the nearest men to take the long-boat and row over to Rivermouth Mountain shore as quickly as possible.

Suddenly Bork lunged so that Tulle was forced to leap up, and Bork rushed at him shouting: 'If you won't fight me, then you'll at least have to run from me!'

And he harried Tulle ahead of him.

Tulle ran along the shore, just quickly enough so that he was always out of Bork's reach, with Bork shouting mockingly behind him. Tulle said nothing. He was stronger and more lithe than Bork, afflicted as he was with neither ale-paunch nor bitter thoughts. 'I'll run until he tires,' he thought. 'Perhaps I can talk him out of it when he is tired.'

And they ran past the bay where Libite had lived with her father. In passing, Tulle turned his head just enough to glimpse the lime woods, black and dense below the mountain. There were fox tracks in the snow. The two of them ran on and came on to the headland with the two old marker pine trees, the sacred pines where Tulle had left his drops of blood. Bork had begun to pant and puff, now shouting only occasional insults about Tulle living with animals and having the heart of a rabbit. Tulle looked round. It sounded as if Bork had begun to weaken. At that moment, Tulle stumbled and fell among the stones, dropping his sword so that he should not cut himself, and rolling right round once.

In a flash he was on his feet again and had grasped Striker, but one of his ankles now pained him so that he could no longer run. He limped over to the marker pines and leant against them.

Bork came closer, grinning all over his face. He held up his sword and pretended to measure it against Striker. 'Which shall I take?' he said.

'Come closer,' said Tulle. 'I'm tired of all this. My

ankle hurts and I wish to go home.' As he said it, he retreated backwards between the trees towards the small pines to give himself some elbow room. He propped his knee against one of them, standing firmly on his good foot, grasping Striker in his hand.

Bork came striding between the sacred pines. At once they began to rustle and sway and creak, then they slid towards each other like the blades of a pair of scissors. Letting out a yelp, Bork tried to fling himself forward. The trunks of the pine trees fastened on his leg, then drew apart again, rustling loudly, but quite still. Bork screamed loudly and then lay groaning.

Tulle stood staring in bewilderment.

Up on Tulaborg hill, Libite stood watching. She had seen the blue cloak flapping along the edge of the water, and the red following, their small greyish-brown companions slightly behind them. She saw the longboat with its six oars racing across the water, its wash foaming behind it.

Tulle came limping home, his arm round Kare's shoulders. Bork came on a stretcher. When his trousers had been cut open, they saw that his leg from knee to ankle was quite shapeless, sore and reddish-blue, with splinters of bone sticking out of it. Tulle said that Halva should see to him. His own injury was nothing but a sprain and would soon be better.

He limped inside, sat down by the hearth and was given hot ale and soup. He said he had lost all desire to go hunting again for a while.

Bork lay unconscious while Halva tended to his crushed leg, but when he regained consciousness, he shrieked so loudly that it disturbed everyone in the hall, so Tulle ordered him to be carried out to the bath-house and housed there for the time being.

Libite bandaged Tulle's ankle with strips of firm linen. She remained kneeling in front of him, his foot in her lap.

'I'm afraid that the spirits on the headland were offended when you refused their help. You should have cut off Bork's head as he lay there, and left it and his sword as an offering. Now we'll have to endure him until he is well again. And he will always be our enemy as long as he lives.'

Tulle morosely agreed that she was probably right.

'But it was so difficult to strike him,' he said 'Because I saw Father Sigulf's face in the air as we ran. When he grew old, it sometimes happened that his eyes watered when he looked at us – at Steinhulf and Bork and me.'

# 6

# YULETIDE

Tile was dreaming that he was in a strange country.

He was walking across a plain with his brothers and sisters and several other children. Grass was growing. He could see occasional clumps of low trees, but they were obscure. The air was thick with a greyish-blue mist, the sky misty, too, and the sun like a glowing coin. On the edge of the plain were huts with people inside them. Tile had asked: 'May we go and play on the plain?' and had received an answer: 'Yes, but you must come home before dark.' The sun was high in the sky. The children played and roamed far out towards the plain, the sun still high in the sky. The children ran about and grew tired and hungry, and the sun *stayed still.* Suddenly Tile noticed that it was not moving at all, and he was gripped by a terrible fear. He called out to his brothers and sisters. At that moment, the sun shrank and became as small as a star, finally disappearing altogether. It was like that in that country. The sun did not set when evening came – but went out. And Tile and the other children, who had not known that beforehand, were left in the dark on the plain.

He woke sobbing, his grief far greater than his fear, his grief for the sun. Then he felt his mother's hand on his face. She slept so lightly that she woke at the slightest twitch, having heard his distress deep down in her own slumbers. Then she lay still again. They were all lying warm and close in the bed, snuffling and breathing with different sounds.

Sometimes when Tile Tulle woke abruptly in the night, he could not remember where he was. He lay there in the dark, knowing nothing but that he was a child who had been dreaming, horribly sometimes, so that his heart wept. He had lived through immeasurable ages in his dream and gone through more than he could bear. Sometimes it seemed to him that everyone he had ever known had died long, long ago. Sometimes he thought his name was Sven and that he had only one hand.

It was not absolutely dark in the chamber. The embers on the hearth were buried, but on one of the hearthstones there was the little tallow candle they called the wolf-eye. They had plenty of seal-oil at that time, so could allow it to burn all night. Soon it would be Yuletide.

After Yuletide, the sun would come back.

He felt better now and settled down. This is how things were – the Lord of the Sky had a daughter who was the Sun Maiden, and she had long shining hair. Hobard had told them. He knew long songs about her and her mother, the dark earth. But Tile could tell the story just as well himself.

The Sun Maiden goes out into the forest – why does she, and what for? Tile had forgotten. She walks along and meets a little old woman who is cold and says: 'Put your warm hand on me! Listen to the chattering of my teeth!' And they walk on together, the old woman tempting the Sun Maiden off the track.

Small fir trees spring up in their tracks, dense prickly little firs shooting up out of the ground. The Sun Maiden's hair gets caught in them and is pulled out, one strand after another. The old woman takes her to a mountain where there is a pass they have to go through, a deep black crevice. And all the time the small pines keep springing up! There is a cave in the mountain, and the old woman says: 'Come in here and rest awhile at my place.' The Sun Maiden replies: 'I'm not tired,' The old woman says: 'Lighten me for a moment, for my cave has never seen the sun.' And she trembles and shakes pleadingly at the Sun Maiden's skirt.

The Sun Maiden goes into the mountain and it closes behind her. The cave inside becomes quite light. But now the whole world outside is as black as night, only the faintest glimmer from the hairs the pines have torn loose showing at midday in the southern sky. The old woman places trolls and demons on guard all round the mountain. The Sun Maiden says from inside the cave: 'Make me a little hole so that I have some air!' The old woman makes a little opening up in the wall with her finger, like the little round window high up in a bath-house ceiling.

Young Svipul, or Sveip as he is also called, has gone out in search of the Sun Maiden. He travels day and night, riding through the darkness, riding through the dark forest, full of trolls and wolves and ice-eagles.

He kills them all.

'One has to remember,' thought Tile, 'never to put a bloodstained sword back into the sheath when it is freezing, because then the sword freezes fast and cannot be drawn when the next enemy comes.'

Sveip sees the glimmering track of hairs on the branches of the pines. And he rides along, collecting up the hairs in his hand. Then he comes to the great mountain with the tiny shining opening and what do the trolls say? They say: 'No one in!'

'One!' he replies.

'*One* gets in,' thought Tile, safe in the warmth of his snuffling brothers and sisters. Some of the trolls fled from Sveip, others he killed. Then he slashed the mountain wall to pieces and beheaded the old woman. He placed the Sun Maiden up behind him on his horse and rode back, the whole world growing lighter and rejoicing as he rode.

To help pay tribute to Sveip, they lit fires in the shape of the sun-cross at Yuletide. Tile well remembered from previous years what they had done – sixteen fires in a circle and a cross of nine inside the circle. They all rode between the fires, slowly at first, then at a gallop. In Tuntula, where hitherto there had been no horses, they went on foot, or ran, with bunches of rye-straw in the left hand and drawn sword

in the right. This year there were horses. Perhaps Tile would try to ride himself. And people sang.

All kinds of things happened that Tile could not quite keep apart. There was a lot of noise, but also great silence, while the torches flared, thrust into the snow round the shrine. There was a lot of tramping back and forth and great preparations. Food was offered to all the spirits and to all their ancestors, but other kinds of spirits were also chased away. Stripped firs with their tops left on were erected in pairs in front of the hall and the cattle-shed. And burning arrows were fired, aimed at the summer and the great wedding time of the sun. 'Bilberry time,' thought Tile, as he lay there, his mouth watering.

But inside the great mountain, the old woman's head slowly rolls towards her stump of neck, and when the head reaches the neck, it grows together again. Then when the time comes, she again lies in ambush. And the Sun Maiden allows herself to be deceived. Has she no memory? Have the gods no memories? Human beings remember, some more than others; that is their heritage.

# 7
# HIS BROTHER LEAVES

The Yuletide slaughter had to be done earlier than usual in Tulaborg that year, because of Bork and his men. Bork himself was a sick man for a long time, so over Yuletide itself, the Tulles were left in peace. But when the days began to lengthen, he started recovering. He became bored and awkward, demanding delicacies such as nuts and honey and cream and fresh meat. But Halva was looking after him, and she displeased him. She was so ugly, he said, and who would know whether she was treating him properly?

'No one,' said King Tulle. 'She knows best.'

The sea-ice was firm as far out as could be seen and King Tulle was able to send Bork's men out seal hunting. Binnab liked it out on the ice. He said it reminded him of his homeland, great wildernesses and strong light. But he was very cold until a pair of sealskin trousers was made for him.

Tulle made an offering of seal-skulls, asking the spirits of the pines what he should do. But they did not answer, neither with signs nor sounds. He thought of going up to Hammerhead Hill and asking the spirit that lived there, but somehow he did not dare be away from home so long.

Bork was learning to walk again, on crutches and supported by Sigge, then on his own. He was also practising riding. One day he let it be known that he wished to speak to Tulle in the hall. Word had gone round all his men, and they had gathered there in their best clothes, their weapons in their hands. When Bork came striding in with his helmet on, his red cloak billowing, they saluted by striking their shields.

'Oh, so things are to be this formal, are they?' said Tulle. He had arrived straight from the smithy at Bork's message, covered with soot, washing himself in the snow outside the door and taking off his leather apron. He called for Hobard and Egil and everyone else within earshot, then went over to the throne, put on his crown and sat down. Libite came and stood beside him. Halva flung an armful of brushwood on to the fire. The sun was very bright that day, the sky dark-blue and the snow blindingly white. The roof-hatch was open, but the hall was fairly dark. The children had been out tobogganing on the slope and came in to watch.

Tulle was waiting for Bork to speak, and Bork was waiting for silence. Then he said:

'I charge you, Tulle, son of thrale woman calling himself king, of inveigling me into a trap by means of witchcraft and magic, so that I shall never be fit again. You have broken the laws of hospitality. And you have refused me my own defence. I demand recompense for the injury my body and my reputation have suffered.'

After he had spoken, he nodded and at that signal, all his men slapped their shields again and let out a growling roar.

'Your behaviour is both offensive and boorish,' replied Tulle, in annoyance. 'It was not by my will that you were injured. If the same thing should happen again, I would certainly behave differently. But I am willing to offer you reasonable recompense, provided I can be sure that you will leave with your men and I need never see you again. You may take back this gold-threaded material that was so fine and expensive.'

Bork grimaced at the material and said: 'I want something useful. I've enough fancy things elsewhere. I want Striker, your sword.'

His escort roared again. Quite silently, between them and the fire, Tile had walked down the length of the row of men, gazing at them and their weapons, and smiling at the ones he knew well. The only one to smile back was Binnab. Tile was six years old now, a strong handsome child. He stopped in front of Bork.

'I do not wish to give you Striker my sword,' said Tulle.

Bork lowered his eyes and said in a calm, quiet voice: 'I intend to wage war on King Steinhulf, who has unjustly taken over the kingdom of Sigga Valley. For such an enterprise, courage and good men are required. And good weapons. I have courage, as everyone knows, and my men are good men, although they've had to work themselves to the bone for nothing here on your land. Your sword, Striker, is better than all other swords, and should rest in a hand that knows how to use it. If you refuse to give it to me, to whom you owe so much, both from this winter and from the past, I have another suggestion. Come to war and fight for me. If you're still alive when Sigga Valley is captured, you're free to go back home with Striker.'

'I do not agree with your suggestion,' said Tulle.

Then Bork leant forward, swiftly lifted Tile and held him on his good knee, at the same time drawing out his long dagger and holding the point at Tile's back.

'I offer you a third possibility,' he said. 'My weapons are, as you know, not quite as good as yours, but they are good enough to stick little pigs. I'll stick this little pig of yours and his blood will suffice as reparation between us.'

Queen Libite had let out a gasp as soon as he had touched Tile. Now she stood tense and trembling beside Tulle, her eyes burning and her teeth bared. 'You were right,' said Tulle sorrowfully to her. 'I should have beheaded him. I should have let you creep in to him and bite his throat.'

Tile struggled, kicking Bork on his still tender knee so that he let out a loud yell and Sigge leapt forward to help hold the boy.

Tulle rose and said in a harsh voice:

'Let my son go and I will agree to go with you to Sigga Valley and fight for you with Striker.'

Bork flung Tile away so that he tumbled over, but he was soon on his feet again, rushing at Bork and biting his hand. Libite called him to her.

Bork said that he wished to leave at once, and there was a great stir in the house and outside as the horses were led out and saddle-bags packed, fodder sacks filled and provisions packed into haversacks.

Tulle took the crown off his head and placed it on Libite's.

'Rule while I am away,' he said.

She looked up into his face, closed her eyes and stroked his cheeks and neck and chest, then scrabbled at him with her hands.

'Don't shoot any foxes on your way,' she said.

'Stay at home,' he said.

She swallowed and promised. 'I'll stay at home. But don't shoot any foxes. Remember, ever since we were married, the fox has been your companion.'

She followed him out. Bork was already mounted and now bowed in the saddle, smiling at her and calling: 'Wish us luck, mistress!' Libite went over to him, her eyes glittering and her mouth in a straight line, and she spoke words to him that were the strongest curse of ill-will – 'North and below,' she said.

It would be impossible to ride through the forest in the deep snow and the cold of the night. But Bork had found out about the ice-route through his men, and reckoned they would be able to get to the fishing village by the mouth of the River Sigga in a day and a night if they rode all the time.

They set off in a long procession. Out on the ice, they fanned out to spread the load. The snow lay hard-packed and radiant in the sunlight. Some of the men had eye-protectors of thin shavings of wood fastened round their heads, and others had to make do with rubbing soot round their eyes. The horses had stood inactive all winter, as Bork had not wished to lend them out for working, so now they frisked and pranced about, snorting. Some wanted to set off at a gallop, but Bork at once put a stop to any such thing. A brisk trot was as much as he allowed, partly so that the ice would not begin to rock and partly because they had a long ride ahead of them.

Tulle was riding a packhorse, fairly close to Bork. He was warmly clad and his blue cloak fluttered outside his fur coat. Although so embittered, he nevertheless found it good to be riding, as he had not been on a horse since he was a boy. But his expression gave nothing away, his face as stiff as wood, and he pretended not to notice when Bork now and again turned round to look at him.

# 8
# TO SIGGA VALLEY

Towards evening, they rode along a shallow shore, in a direction that meant they had the setting sun behind them and the rising moon ahead of them. The ice along the shore had burst several times during the course of the winter, pressing up the flood water into frozen shiny patches, with protruding ridges in between. These patches reflected the bluish green colour of the moon, and the crusty ridges were flame-yellow on the sun side and violet in the shadows. The strips of cloud above them were red and blue against the blue-green sky. As the party rode on, the ridges reddened, the sky ahead turning a darker blue and the moon shining. The colours were so strong that they caused a sense of dizziness, a gripping sense of fear, as if they were all entering the reception hall of a powerful ruler, unexpected and uninvited.

But they rode on and came out on to the open sea-ice again. The sun sank, taking the flaring colours down with it below the horizon. The moon rose. There were more islands here, and they rode in and out between the long shadows.

Tulle rode with his head lowered, warming one hand at a time under his clothes, holding the reins with the other. At one time, Sigge came over to him and said: 'King Bork sends his greetings and asks what kind of dogs they are you have with you?'

Tulle raised his head and saw long slim shadowy figures running alongside. 'I brought no dogs with me,' he replied to Sigge.

They rode on, icicles in their beards, Tulle again and again glancing down and to the sides, each time glimpsing those swift shadowy figures with tails. He pretended not to see them. The small rough-haired horses turned white with rime-frost. Sigge reined in his horse and when he was alongside Tulle, he said: 'King Bork sends his greetings and says send home your dogs.'

Tulle did not even look up. 'I have no dogs to send home,' he said.

The night turned very cold. They rode across the ice in the grey moonlight, occasionally dismounting and walking for a while, running and jumping so that they would not stiffen up completely. Once they stopped for a rest on a wooded island.

Bork flung himself swearing off his horse and sat down on a pile of furs Sigge had spread out, allowing himself to be rubbed and fortified with ale from a horn that had been carried beneath clothes so that it had not frozen. He issued no orders. The men had been on winter journeys before and knew what to do.

They gathered firewood, swept a place clear and lit

a fire. They found stones on the shore and heated them in the fire, then unloaded the two large wooden troughs from the back of the packhorses and filled them with snow. When the stones were hot, they were raked out of the fire and put into the snow-filled troughs. Then they were exchanged as soon as they had cooled. Snow was added all the time, so they soon had drinking water for the horses, and Binnab added a few pinches of salt to it, although the others laughed at him and called him wasteful.

They stamped round the fire, munching their food, but no one except Bork dared sit down in case they fell asleep. They drank ale from horns with wooden lids and plugs at the narrow end, that they had been carrying beneath their clothes. Tulle had no sack of food with him. He had not even thought of such a thing when he had left Tuntula, so he secretly chewed pine-needles. But Binnab gave him bread and dried meat. 'Eat,' he said. 'It's yours.' He smiled at Tulle, and Tulle smiled back and accepted the food.

During the next stretch, from midnight to dawn, Tulle had strange dreams. His back and legs were aching terribly from riding for the first time for so long. He knew that he was riding on and on, that the night was widespread and iron-grey all round, but at the same time he sensed a rustling and a whispering of pale green leaves and flowers as well as Libite's presence. He spoke silently to her and called her everything beautiful he could think of – wild-honey, birch-sap, wild strawberry.

Then dawn came, pink and blue, the world again becoming coloured, the moon fading. The sun hurt their eyes. The horses' heads hung right down to the snow and it seemed as if they had all, horse and man, grown great ice humps on their backs. They moved slowly, but they moved, and they all arrived alive at the fishing village at the mouth of the Sigga.

Bork swung groaning off his horse and allowed himself to be helped into the largest hut, shouting hoarsely for hot ale and a place to sleep.

The fishing village was not large, only four or five hovels with outhouses round about. Only women and children and animals were at home, as well as a few old men. Bork's men were all found a place, tucked into beds and packed into hay on floors. It was worse for the the horses, but somehow room was found for them all among the pigs and sheep, lined up close, side touching side against the frosty wall.

Just before he fell asleep, Bork said: 'Tulle, son of thrale woman . . . and one other . . . can stand guard . . . until we wake . . .'

Sigge, who was sitting at the head of his bed, repeated the order. 'King Bork sends his greetings . . .' Snores were already resounding from all directions. Tulle stepped over the bodies lying on the floor and went out. He shook himself in the cold sunlight, picked up a handful of snow and rubbed his face with it.

A woman looked out from the nearest cattle shed. 'Come and have some milk,' she said. 'Not that there's much at this time of year.'

'Who are you?' he said, after he had emptied the pail. 'I seem to know you.'

'I am Asta. I lived in the king's domain when I was a child, so we've played together. But I married and live here now. We've heard strange rumours about you. Is it true that you've entered into an alliance with the trolls?'

'Hm,' said Tulle. 'Where is your husband?'

'He and all the other men are with King Steinhulf. He gathered an army together just before Yuletide. We don't know what's happened to them. Why don't you sleep?'

Tulle replied that he was on guard-duty.

Asta snorted. 'You sleep,' she said. 'I'll wake you if anything happens.'

Then Binnab came tottering out, saying he wished to stand guard with Tulle. Asta led them to a small outhouse and helped them bury themselves in the hay and dry reeds. She had hardly turned her back when small lithe furry animals leapt in and curled themselves up on top of them. They warmed them well. Tulle and Binnab fell asleep and slept until Asta came and woke them at dusk. Then the animals had gone, but a sharp scent remained in the hay.

Bork made his presence felt in the fishing village, his leg hurting and himself irritable. He ordered food to be brought, but turned up his nose at what was provided, dried and salt fish and frozen seal-meat. On his orders, the men slaughtered a cow and a pig, neither Asta nor anyone else in the village able to stop them. He was angry when he heard there was no more ale, and had Sigge boil rich blood-soup with onions and salt instead. Then he summoned Asta to him, as well as old Toll, who was Asta's father-in-law, and asked them what had happened in Sigga Valley lately.

At the same time, Sigge was in the next hovel asking the same questions of the other women. Binnab was ordered to question all the children, but did not wish to. He protested that he had a cold and could not speak.

Bork was told no more than what Asta had already told Tulle, that Steinhulf had summoned all the men capable of bearing arms to his domain. He had had scouts sent north, west and east. No, no one knew King Steinhulf's plans. No, King Steinhulf was not one to confide in anyone.

Bork stroked his beard that Sigge had had to burnish and groom before the meal. His stomach was full and he felt more contented now. 'There is no doubt,' he said, 'that Steinhulf fears that I will attack. From the north or the west or the east. He has taken the men of the country out of my reach.' Bork began to laugh softly, his stomach shaking. 'He always was short-sighted, my brother,' he said. 'He has left me the women.'

There was a short silence, but then Asta cried angrily, 'We'd rather stick knives into ourselves than fight against our own men!' She tried to leap at Bork, but Sigge and a man by the name of Tume grabbed her quickly by the arms. She spat.

'Good woman,' said Bork, with no sign of anger. 'You misunderstand me. You will not be fighting. But you will dress as men and follow my retinue to increase its visible strength. We'll march to the king's domain and halt at a discreet distance. I myself and a few men will ride up and challenge Steinhulf. He will wilt at the sight of my power . . .'

'Steinhulf has never wilted in his life!' hissed Asta.

'Good woman,' said Bork again. 'Let me finish. His army consists of your men – fathers, husbands, sons. Do you think *they* will want to fight against *you*? No, they'd prefer to stick knives into themselves. With no bloodshed, you will paralyse the evil power of King Steinhulf. The country will be liberated from danger by gentle female hands. Steinhulf will be forced to fight me alone at last – against one man from my retinue, as I am at present lame – or give up and submit completely.'

He talked and talked thus, his mouth as smooth as cream, and brought the women over on to his side. The following day, they cut off their plaits and made them into beards, then cut their skirts in half and made them into trousers. They wound sealskin round their legs and tied knives to poles as spears. Some of them had ice-picks and seal-irons.

All this time Tulle said nothing, and no one spoke to him except Binnab and Asta.

Then, bedded down in a sledge with Sigge as driver, Bork preceded his retinue along the River Sigga. Half his men rode behind the sledge. Then came the women in a line in pairs – followed by the remaining horsemen with Tulle and the packhorses. Only old Toll and the children and a few ancient old women were left behind in the fishing-village, with the animals Bork had not had slaughtered. Some of the women wept as they walked, their tears freezing on to their beards, but no one looked round.

# 9
# THE KING'S DOMAIN

Bork gathered up all the women from the farms and villages as he went on, and he sent Tume and some others up into the forests to make his case in places he had no time to visit. If any of them were not tempted by his words, he did as he had done in Tulaborg; threatened to knife their children, as the country was in danger, he said, and he had that message passed on. Thus he acquired a retinue that at a distance looked terrifyingly large.

It was a strange feeling for Tulle, riding through the country, for he had not been there for twenty years, and it was smaller than he remembered.

The king's domain lay on the south bank of the Sigga, between stone hills that were not particularly high, but were very steep. Bork approached from the south, at first along the river, then diagonally across the open river meadows that were marshy and difficult terrain in the summer. He made his flock halt at a suitable distance from the palisade and ordered them to stand as still as possible where he had placed them. Then he selected his best and most loyal men to go with him to the gateway. He was grimacing with tension, licking his lips and mumbling, having prepared several different speeches. 'If Steinhulf says *this*, then we'll say *that*. If on the other hand he says *that*, then we'll say *this*. Sigge and Tume behind me with spears at the ready. Tulle between Are and Kettil. Have Striker at the ready. You're the one who will fight Steinhulf in my place, as you destroyed my leg.'

He looked sharply at Tulle. Tulle's face remained expressionless. They marched up to the gateway.

When they had come within twenty paces, it opened and out tumbled Odrik the steward, half-dressed and his arms outstretched. 'Bork, King Bork! Praise be to Tinderas! Hurry in with your men. You've come just in time, there are practically no men in the fortress. King Steinhulf went north to meet the Kiralas, but they were more than we thought. Some of them surrounded him and held him there in the forest. Another lot came south – they have skis and move faster than a horse can run on flat ground. They fly over the snow, especially at night, and aren't affected by the cold. They live off the bark of trees when they're not eating human flesh. I've just had a message from the wife of Grim, whose holding is down by the river Rodde, and they say they're ravaging and burning in Rodde. She sent her youngest son with the message.'

Bork grimaced terrifyingly. Odrik wrung his old hands. His trembling old voice was not strong, but the women had understood all the same and started wailing: 'The Kiralas! The Kiralas! We must get back home!' And began running away.

Bork sprang into action, holding up both arms and bellowing like thunder:

'Halt! If you go back to your farms, the Kiralas will butcher you one and all. If you stay here, you can still save all. Stop the Kiralas and hinder their progress. Tempt them into gathering here until King Steinhulf gets out and can surround them. We shall do that, and then we have captured them. We'll crush all the Kiralas' best men to death and then we'll have peace for ever afterwards.'

Odrik wrung his hands in confusion when the women began pouring past him through the gateway. 'But your men? Where are your men, King Bork?'

'Women are better than men in besieged fortresses,' said Bork, fingering his beard. 'They eat less, and they fight more fiercely, because they want to get back to their brats. Take them to the rear yard and have them practice with bows and arrows, Odrik.'

He began to arrange for the defence of the fortress, but he was confused and angry, saying that his leg ached so that he couldn't think. It was clear that the women could not be trained in one afternoon, even if there had been enough bows and arrows for them all. Some of them wept so that their sight was impaired, and their hands and feet were stiff with cold.

Tulle went over to Bork and said: 'I promised to fight for you with Striker, but if the Kiralas shoot burning arrows as they usually do, I'm not likely to have the opportunity.'

'Don't think I'll let you go home because of that,' grunted Bork.

'I want you to hand over the leadership to me for a while,' said Tulle.

Bork grunted again. Tulle was leaning on his sword. 'Oh well,' said Bork irritably, adopting an expression of inscrutability and turning to Odrik: 'Let Tulle take command until I say "enough".'

Tulle placed some of the weaker women on guard up on the wooden towers. Everyone else inside the fortress was set to work drawing water from the well and pouring it slowly over the palisade, the walls and roofs, as slowly as possible. It was laborious work, but he allowed them to rest in shifts and gave them drinks of hot meat-stock that was constantly boiling in a pot.

When dusk fell, it grew colder, and then even the most foolish began to understand what he was doing. The whole of the fortress was covered with an armour of ice glittering in the torchlight.

Tulle was working down on the ice. He drew his sword and hacked at the ice as hard as he could. The ice cover broke beneath his blows; the greatest miracle the men had ever seen. The ice was a good ell thick, but he chopped it like wood, no, like cheese, some of them said later. He hacked out blocks and had them dragged down to the shore. He hacked away and made the men build a wall of ice-blocks as an outer palisade below the fortress. The hole he cut out grew wider and wider, steaming in the cold, but the steam thinned out gradually as the water froze over again.

The moon rose and Tulle went back into the fortress with his men and horses, for now there was nothing to do but wait.

They all sat or lay down in the straw on the floor round the fire. Those who could, slept. Many of them could not. The women twisted and turned, some of them weeping, rustling as they turned restlessly, sighing and talking about their children.

King Tulle had sat down by the door of the women's house and was talking to Asta. She had kept her courage up for quite a long time, but as the evening progressed, she grew more and more silent, looking at Tulle with such an expression in her eyes that he himself felt surly and unhappy. He went over to the house the men had been stowed in and found them all wide awake, telling yarns. A man called Odde was in the middle of a story about how he had been flung on to the shore of a nameless island off the coast after a shipwreck . . .

In the confusion of voices that followed after his story, when many of them at once tried to tell of similar events that had happened to them, they did not at first hear the women on guard shrieking – Tulle was the first to run out and up the north tower. The women were shrieking: 'They're not the Kiralas – they're wolves!' Then someone else cried: 'The Kiralas are werewolves, every one of them.'

The moon had risen, but was still low in the sky, so the shadows were long and it was hard to distinguish anything. Tulle cupped his hands round his eyes.

Dark patches were flitting across the snow, coming closer and closer. 'Stop!' he shouted, when a man beside him put an arrow to his bow. 'They're not wolves. They're foxes. Don't waste good arrows on a fox.'

'I've never heard of foxes hunting in a pack,' said the man who had been about to shoot. 'I'll go down and see for myself,' said Tulle. And he did. He opened the gate in the palisade just wide enough to allow him to slip through, then closed it behind him. He could be heard talking. Then he came back in. 'Put out all the torches now,' he said. 'The Kiralas are coming.'

He sent the women up on to the footbridge that ran round the inner edge of the palisade, telling them to hold their spears ready. They were not to throw them, but use them as daggers and thrusting weapons should the Kiralas happen to surmount the obstacles he had set up and begin to climb. He himself went down and hid himself behind the ice wall with about ten men. Then the Kiralas came.

They swarmed in from the forest by the river Rodde, like a swarm of wintery midges, firing burning arrows. But the arrows did not stick in the slippery ice. They simply slid away and fell hissing into the snow. The women up on the bridge could not help jeering and shaking their spears. The Kiralas retreated, swinging round, leaping easily on their skis, holding their ski-sticks under their left arms to have their hands free for their weapons. Their leader called out and the

whole long line of them again came in to attack. They had the moonlight in their eyes and could not distinguish the ice wall from the snow-covered shore below the fortress. Neither did they see the hole in the ice. They flew on towards it at such a speed that they had no time to stop, even when they heard the new ice cracking. They swung round, flinging themselves to right and left, knocking each other over and sinking into the water among the clinking ice. 'Now!' said Tulle to his men, and they came out and struck the Kiralas over the head with the great wooden clubs they had whittled during the evening. They struck until there was no more sound from the water, not another single splash.

Tulle left his men to haul out the dead Kiralas and put them in a heap inside the ice-wall. He told them to cut spruces and lay them along the edge of the ice-hole. Then he went back to the fortress. Bork had been standing watching everything from the tower. He came down and went over to Tulle.

'Sigga Valley is mine,' he said.

'Until Steinhulf comes,' said Tulle. 'He's heading this way, in the tracks of the Kiralas. He was after them, which was why they were in such a hurry. They wanted to get here before he did.'

'How do you know that?' said Bork.

Tulle did not reply.

'Insolent pup!' said Bork. 'Although I allowed you to win this battle on your own, instead of taking the honour myself, you're still insolent. Tell me!'

Tulle snorted.

Bork blew out his cheeks, straightened up and slapped his leather-gloved hands together. 'I will now take command over the fortress! Remove the spruces at once and hide them behind the wall.'

'If they do that, then Steinhulf will also be in danger of falling in,' said Tulle.

'Not so fast, boy,' said Bork. 'You've fought for me with Striker, and when Steinhulf has fallen through the ice and drowned, you will be free to go home to your lair, if you're still alive then, of course. You pledged me your loyalty of your own free will, instead of letting the blood of a little pig once and for all wash away our differences . . .'

'. . . what difference does it make to you,' he went on, 'whether you strike him down with your sword or he falls through the ice that you have yourself cut open with it?'

Tulle was tired and shook his head.

'There is a difference,' he said. 'Of course there's a difference. I'll go down to the ice-hole and wait for Steinhulf there.'

They had been standing talking to each other in the middle of the fortress. Behind Bork stood Sigge and Tume. Behind Tulle stood no one at all. Binnab was at work with the other men down by the ice-hole. Asta was on the footbridge, in the flock of women, stamping and hopping about to keep themselves warm.

Tulle swung round to go, and at a quick signal from Bork, Sigge and Tume leapt forward and hit

Tulle over the head. They caught him under his arms as he fell and dragged him into the hall. 'What's happened?' said a woman they met, and Bork replied: "Tulle's been wounded . . . put him down by the fire,' he went on to Sigge and Tume.

As Tulle lay unconscious and Bork was ordering the women in, Binnab was going to the cookhouse with eight dry sticks under his arm. He set them alight at the hearth and went out again with them. No one who saw him gave another thought to why he had done so. He stood by the gateway and lit the men's way in as they came from their work down by the ice-hole. Then he thrust all eight torches into the drifts outside the palisade. Afterwards, he said he had heard Tulle's voice telling him to do that.

Bork had ordered everyone to go to bed, and most fell asleep the moment their heads were down. He himself remained on the seat of honour, Tulle opposite him, groaning as he recovered consciousness, then holding his head in his hands and vomiting so that the fire hissed.

'Take a little ale,' said Bork with a grin. He was pleased. 'Sigge and Tume are up in the tower.'

Tulle rinsed out his mouth with ale and felt no better for it. The floor was covered with snoring men now, the sound making his head hurt, just as the firelight stung his eyes.

Tume came in and said in a low voice to Bork: 'There's something peculiar on the ice, a great many small lights gliding over the snow.'

'Is it Steinhulf?' said Bork.

'We can't see any men. All we can see are flares swaying back and forth along the ice-hole. We heard a kind of tramping farther away, a crunching in the snow, but now all is quiet.'

'Will-o'-the-wisps,' said Bork, with a belch. 'The Kiralas haven't got used to being dead yet. Go on back up to the tower.'

Tume went out and returned again to say that all was quiet now, apart from himself and Sigge, only Odrik was awake.

'Odrik's an old fool. Go on back up – no, get me some more ale first.'

Tume went out and came back again. 'We can hear the crunching of many men's feet in the snow,' he said. 'But we can see no men. All we can see is something strange – a piece of snow moving – a shadow running forward. No, not the shadow of a man, nor of an animal, either. I can't say what it looks like – and the will-o'-the-wisps have gone.'

'You aren't afraid of ghosts, are you, Tume?'

'They say that the Kiralas practise magic.'

'Turn the edge of your knife towards the wind.'

'There's no wind tonight.'

'Send an arrow towards the shadow then, one with a rune on its shaft. Take this one. It's painted with wolf's blood.'

Tume went out.

There were voices outside. Odrik's old voice

sounded excited. But then it was silent, silent for a long time. The fire sputtered and the men snored.

Bork gulped down ale and the straw on the floor rustled when anyone moved.

Then the door flew open and Sigge came in, moving quickly. Once by Bork's seat, he opened his mouth to speak, but then stopped with a jerk. Then he raised the old shield of iron that had belonged to King Sigulf, the shield Tulle had carried all the way but had found no use for. Sigge went down on one knee and held it below Bork's face. 'Look and see if I've polished it well, as you bade me to,' he said, his voice hoarse.

Bork was heavy with ale. He leant forward and looked into the shield as if it were a mirror. He sighed deeply, his whole body heaving, and then said slowly:

'You've polished it well, Sigge.' Then he went on in a louder voice: 'Tulle, you did put those spruces by the ice-hole as I ordered, didn't you? I'm anxious about my brother. I shall go down to the ice myself.' He rose, took a few steps, but then stumbled, almost falling into the fire.

'What nonsense you talk,' said Tulle angrily, opening his eyes. They were smarting again. He saw a flaming sword raised in the dim light behind the seat. Then he saw a firelit hand. A leather arm. A dim figure. Someone had come quite silently in through the back way and was standing there, unheard through all the rustling, snoring and sputtering. It was Steinhulf.

Bork had seen him reflected in the shield, and once

again was pretending innocence. He straightened up his fat body and headed towards the door, staggering drunkenly. 'Come, Sigge,' he said loudly, as he leant against the wall, just managing to remain on his feet, the door opening in front of him as if of its own accord.

Steinhulf sat down on the seat of honour, his sword unsheathed across his knees.

'Sigge,' he said. Sigge stopped on his way out. 'Sigge, do you wish to save the honour of your master?'

Sigge looked over his shoulder and grimaced wearily. 'Isn't it too late, King Steinhulf?'

'You have remained loyal and followed your master faithfully and far. Do so for a little while longer. It is cold tonight.'

Sigge left. Steinhulf sat quite still on the seat of honour, Tulle lay flat on his back with the fire between them. After a while, Tulle said in a sleepy voice: 'How did you get here? Did you see my brothers-in-law with flares in their mouths?'

'I saw foxes running with torches in their mouths. My men were frightened. We made a detour round Cairn Mountain, across the Sigga and south of Bear Island. We fastened our cloaks together so that we had a kind of sail. Each man put snow in his mouth and melted it, then sprayed the melted snow on to his cloak. Before it froze again, we threw loose snow on to it. So we had a roof to carry above us, stiff and white and glittering, barely visible against the snow. Neither Sigge nor Tume saw us from the tower. What else do you want to know?'

'I want to know who lit the flares,' said Tulle faintly. 'I did not have time to do it myself.'

Steinhulf just shook his head.

After another long spell, Tulle said indifferently and distantly: 'We were to have fought over Sigga Valley, you and I, in single combat. I on behalf of Bork and you on your own behalf. Now it will be simpler. You can kill me at once.'

Steinhulf leant over towards him and said: 'Is your mind wandering?'

'I knew you were on your way,' said Tulle indistinctly. 'But I dreamt . . .' Then he opened his eyes wide and blinked. 'Steinhulf,' he said in amazement. 'Are you here? That's good, then you can stop everyone pulling at my cloak. They have pulled me over and I have no energy to rise again.'

'It seems,' said Steinhulf, 'that you have given me quite a number of lives, and maybe even my own, whether in a dream or by magic. I will give you your life back in return.'

'I accept your gift,' said Tulle. 'But I don't think it will last for long.' Then he grew confused again and said: 'Steinhulf, are you there? My head's bursting and flaring. I cannot see you. Is Sigga Valley taken? Am I already dead?'

'Sigga Valley is taken,' replied Steinhulf.

# 10

# KING BORK'S HONOUR

Bork walked unsteadily to the ice-hole, drunk and extremely frightened, his breath coming like thick mist from his mouth. He stood staring at the ice-wall and the dead Kiralas for a while, then spat. Water had been poured over them, freezing them into one single block of ice to protect them from wolves. Wolf-howls had been heard earlier that night, but now it was quiet. No, not absolutely quiet. There was a humming and tingling – either in the air or inside his head. He looked up and at once the stars began to swarm round him like midges or gnats. He was forced to close his eyes and lean against the ice-wall.

The snow crunched and he looked round to see Sigge plodding over towards him. 'What are you going to do, King Bork?' he said.

Bork's thoughts were scattering away in all directions, and he had to make an effort to collect them together and keep them inside his skull. 'We'll stay here for a while,' he said. 'Then we'll go and greet Steinhulf with joyous relief and say that we've been waiting anxiously . . .'

'You did not part friends last autumn . . .'

'We'll say that we heard about the ravages of the Kiralas, and decided to forget all previous injustices he'd been the cause of. We have hastened to his aid for the sake of the country.'

'One cannot eat one's own words too often.'

'Odrik received us as friends.'

'Odrik is old and forgetful. He greeted Steinhulf just now with your father's name.'

Bork was silent for a moment. 'How many of my men can I trust?' he asked.

'You can trust me. And Tume. The others . . . I don't know,' said Sigge, shrugging his shoulders. 'They've had to go without pay for so long. You should have let them go free in Tuntula. You should have killed Tulle as soon as we got there, then let them ravage as they pleased.'

'Perhaps it's not yet too late,' said Bork.

Sigge let out an annoyed, barking laugh. 'It is too late. Didn't you see Queen Libite's eyes? When she came out into the sun to bid us farewell. May ill-fortune go with you, she said.'

'She's a troll-cony,' said Bork. 'She's the one who broke my fortune.'

'Huh,' said Sigge. 'Oh, no she isn't. You've been striding along with fire in your feet. It is you who has set fire to the country, and all lands you've walked on are blackened. If you want to go on, then you must find ways you've never walked before.'

'Sigge,' said Bork, his voice more eager now. 'You

were once married to a Kirala woman – is it true when they say that the Kiralas can forge together broken fortunes?'

Sigge stamped up and down, slapping his hands against each other. He was thoughtful. 'They don't talk about fortune as we do,' he said. 'Nor about honour, either. They spit on their arrows before they fire them. They conjure up whatever weather or quarry they wish for. Their women are borne on the wind like trolls. Yes, perhaps there is a way for them when all others are put to the stake.'

He went over to the heap of dead Kiralas and began to look at them one by one.

'What are you looking for?' said Bork.

'Their chieftain. He should have a token round his neck, a carved piece of bone on a thong . . .'

Sigge hacked at the ice with his knife, prising the frozen bodies apart and turning them over one by one. Bork propped his back against the ice-wall. Sigge looked up at him. 'Rest for a while, King Bork,' he said, the cold making his face so stiff that it was hard to speak. 'You're tired.'

'Yes, I'm tired.'

'Are you cold?'

'No, it feels warmer . . .'

'Rest a while,' said Sigge again, rubbing his face hard in his gloves. 'We'll take a pair of the Kiralas' skis each. You can hang the chieftain's insignia round your neck. We'll got to Kirala country and tell them about the battle. They'll have plenty of lone women now, so we'll no doubt be well received . . .'

'They'd kill us,' said Bork. He sounded drowsy.

'They won't kill the person who comes with the chieftain's insignia . . .' Sigge went on, talking for a while, but receiving no reply. He found the chieftain of the Kiralas, a slightly built man with black hair, in a fur tunic like all the others, but with the carved bone-ornament frozen fast to his cheek. He put the bodies back where the had lain before, mumbling a verse over them, Kiralan words he had learnt from his wife, and then he raised his voice: 'King Bork!'

There was no reply. Bork was standing still, hunched up against the ice-wall. Sigge went over and looked into his face, which was white, the eyes closed, ice on the moustache. Sigge nudged him, then nudged harder. Bork fell over and lay still.

Sigge thrust the bone-ornament under his own tunic. Then he took Bork by the feet and slowly began to drag him towards the fortress. Halfway there, Tume came to meet him. 'Go in and get warm,' he said. 'You're almost frozen stiff yourself.' Sigge refused with a grunt. Together, they dragged Bork over the last bit, laying him beside the gateway and covering him with their cloaks.

The next day, they announced that King Bork had died of cold while trying to warn his brother, King Steinhulf, about the ice-hole. Steinhulf nodded and said that he would have Bork buried in keeping with him being the son of a king and a king himself, as soon as spring came and the earth thawed so that it was possible to dig. He had him sewn into a hide and placed in an earthen hideout for the time being. He also asked what Sigge and Tume and the rest of Bork's retinue were now going to do. Most of them chose to go straight into service with Steinhulf. But some wished to go east, to the ruler of Kars country, which was at war with the cannibals and the dog-headed people. Others wished to go back to their farms, where there was more space than before, as so many fathers and elder brothers had been killed. And Sigge joined the Kiralas.

# 11

# ODDE'S TALE

Odde told his tale by the fire in the hall of the king's domain, while they were all waiting for the Kiralas' attack. His ship had been wrecked in a sudden storm and he had been thrown ashore on a small island.

'There was a little shelter there and I crept inside it. There were pines and juniper bushes all round, and crowberries and moss, but otherwise bare smooth rocks, not a stem of chives to be seen, as it was late summer. I was so hungry that I couldn't sit still. I went out into the storm again, right down to the spray and said aloud: 'If only a bit of edible green would come ashore!' And immediately a cabbage was thrown at me.'

The men laughed.

'I got a fire going in the shelter,' Odde went on, 'I heated cooking-stones and boiled the cabbage in a crevice, taking the water to it in my shoes. And then I ate the lot and got a bad stomach. So I went out into the storm again and said aloud: "If only something good to drink would come!" Immediately a keg of the strongest mead was washed ashore.'

'And then?' said the men.

'I drank,' said Odde. 'I sat in the shelter beside the fire and drank. And the storm raged. I felt lonely and said aloud: "If only someone would come to cheer . . ." Then I heard a very faint noise, and there in front of me was a woman. She had long hair hanging loose all round her, and she was wearing nothing but a pair of hide trousers.'

'Then?' said the men eagerly.

'I cannot reveal any more,' said Odde.

They began to shout with disappointment, but one of them was scornful and cried: 'We can imagine the rest!'

'Yes, that'd be better,' said Odde, laughing quietly. Then he raised his voice again. 'I can tell you one more thing. I was rescued later, by men in a fishing boat. And the moment I went on board, they said: "Did you see *her*?"'

# 12

# BINNAB'S TALE

Tulle lay ill and Steinhulf put a man to watch over him; Binnab, as he had requested the task.

Tulle's illness was such that his head ached as soon as he got up. He could not even bear to lie propped up in bed, as flames flashed across his vision and he felt sick. But if he lay still, he felt quite well. They talked together quite a lot, Tulle and Binnab. Once Tulle said: 'Why did you leave your country?'

Binnab did not answer immediately, them muttered that there were no words to say it with. Then he went on to say that it was a sorrowful story. He would try to sing it. But the song hurt Tulle's ears so much that he asked him to stop. After a while, Binnab said he would ponder on his story in silence and see if in time he could make it into something tellable.

'To tell to your grandchildren, O, Tulle King,' he said.

'Why do you say that?' said Tulle.

'I want to go with you to Tuntula and be your man,' said Binnab.

When Tulle was weary and found time dragging, Binnab told him the tale of Turrut-Hisan.

'An immeasurably long time ago, there was a town called Turrut in the Land of the Rivers. The ruler of this town loved gardens and laid down many. He steered the rivers through the town, and thought out clever ways of arranging the watering, even up on the roofs. The houses there were built of clay, both fired and unfired. They were square and had flat roofs covered with pitch and soil, where plants and even trees could grow. In the Land of the Rivers, the sun is hotter than here, and the wind dries out the land. The summer is not a good time, but a hard time and water is short. The ruler strove with his gardens, but was never satisfied.

'In the Land of the Rivers they knew the art of communicating with the stars. The ruler had his own star-watching tower that was higher than all other buildings. Up there in the tower, he stood night after night, calling on the stars and speaking to them. Now story-tellers part ways a little here, so it is hard to know whether they were gods or others living among the stars who came – or whether it was the stars themselves taking on human form. They were translucently white, with strong dark eyebrows and large eyes, and hair like fish-scales or flat mussel shells. For centuries afterwards, the stone-carvers of Turrut tried to reproduce their faces, and carvings of them can still be found in the soil today. But the expression in their eyes is unbearable, although they are only of stone. They are usually quickly buried again, with testimonies of worship.

'The ruler asked the star people for help, and they promised to make a garden for him. It was to stretch right round the town, like a wreath, and a stream of clear water would flow through it. There would be flowers that no one had ever seen before, as well as frogs that could sing.

'The star people worked in the wet clay and the dry dust, sowing seeds they had brought with them under their nails, and they drew furrows with their feet. When they had finished, there was no sign whatsoever of their labours, except the ground was slightly disturbed. "Have patience," they said. "Our seeds and seedlings and arrangements go by our time, which is different from yours." Then they went home again, and the years went by and the ruler never saw anything grow where they had sown.

'Never, never – the time went by, more years than anyone can count, and Turrut was abandoned. The art of living with the stars was lost. Evil winds blew death across the land, rivers overflowed and covered it with silt. Other winds came and blew life into it, so that grass grew among the ruins of ancient cities, and herds of sheep grazed in royal palaces. Gradually new towns were built on the foundations of the old ones, and after a stretch of time so long that the constellations in the sky had changed, a town called Hisan lay where Turrut had previously been.

'All the houses in Hisan were as high as the star-watching tower, and the people lived as close together as bees and ants. A road was built round the town, wide enough for six wagons abreast. It was laid with stones and covered with pitch, and day and night the ground shook with the pounding of vehicles. It was so crowded with beasts of burden and wagons, that at a distance it looked like a snake perpetually creeping along on the spot.

'One day, the garden of the stars burst out! Trees grew up between the houses and through the floors, filling all the rooms! They grew thickly and richly and swiftly, just as when one gets out of bed in the morning! And great cracks that grew wider and wider appeared in the road, the water bubbling blue, water that was blue and wonderful. Great frogs leapt singing into the air, some with water-lilies in their mouths. For the water-lilies of the stars had grown so quickly that their stalks had become tangled, but the frogs helped them all up into daylight. The frogs were as big as sheep, as pink as roses, too, they were, and green like leaves, and they sang like the bird with a thousand tongues. The water-lily leaves were as large as shields, and the water-lilies themselves were different, some like dishes and some like pitchers.

'The people of Hisan town hurled stones and gravel into the water and tried to patch the cracks over with pitch. They tried filling the water-course and pulling up the bushes, cutting down the trees, tearing things down, exterminating them, chasing them away. But it was the garden's day now, and their efforts were in vain.'

# 13
# TO TUNTULA

King Steinhulf wished to marry for the second time and proposed to a royal daughter of a small kingdom that lay east of the East Half of Sigga Valley. He muttered about a foreign cloth with gold threads in it that he wished to send to his bride-to-be as a gift. He had received the cloth from the south and had bartered it for a considerable number of marten-skins. Then it had disappeared during the feud with Bork, and he was afraid it had been burnt, alongside so many other things.

Of Steinhulf's children, only two boys and a girl had survived childhood diseases and hungry winters and grown to adulthood, but the boys had both died at the hands of the Kiralas. The daughter, Steingerd, had married and lived in Ullby, south-west of the king's domain. She had three small sons. She sent a message through Tume, whom she had taken into her service, that if the gold-threaded cloth came to light, it was hers. Steinhulf had promised it to her the previous winter, long before he had even thought of marrying again.

Steinhulf was eager to be rid of Tulle as soon as he

was well again. He equipped both him and Binnab with food and good clothes. Tulle had thought it wiser not to claim the old iron shield, but Steinhulf pressed it on him, saying: 'You have no inheritance from our father.' Tulle would have preferred a horse, but Steinhulf spoke of the decimation of the country. Many horses had first of all been lost during the feud with Bork, secondly sacrificed for good fortune in battle, and thirdly stolen and eaten by the Kiralas. But he promised to send a small herd to Tuntula as soon as he could, three or four, or two, as soon as circumstances permitted.

It was almost spring. The midday thaw made walking heavy going and all south-facing slopes were clear of snow. Tulle and Binnab set off on skis one evening, as the snow-crust then bore their weight. The moon was waxing. They came to the village at the mouth of the Sigga early in the morning, and crept into the same barn as before to sleep. Tulle hung up his shield on the door to show who had come.

They were woken by Asta late in the afternoon. She bade them come into her hut, saying she had food ready for them. 'I see,' she said to Tulle, 'that you still have the shield. Has it been good to you? Didn't you know,' she went on, 'That it is tied to your family's destiny. It brings good or ill-fortune to its bearer, but no one knows which beforehand. It cannot be disposed of unless it is presented as a gift to someone who accepts it of his own free will. It proved to be unlucky for your father. Yes, indeed. He threw it into the sea. Far, far away it flew, skimming over the water, then turned and came back, equally swiftly, striking your father, so that he fell there on the shore. We saw it happen. Then he took the shield and said that if it was the shield's destiny to harden him, then it was probably his destiny to endure.'

As they sat round the fire in Asta's hut, eating seal-meat and seal-blood paste and bread made of reed-roots and bark, she asked them where they were going.

'Home to Tuntula,' said Tulle. 'Will the ice hold?'

'It's beginning to be unsafe,' said Asta's husband, who was back home now.

'Perhaps it'd be best if we went along the shore . . .'

'There's a bunch of Kiralas round about here. We think they escaped from the battle for the king's domain. But we don't understand why they don't go back home. We've a lookout up on Beacon Mountain, so they won't surprise us if they come this way. But we just hope they'll go away.'

Tulle thought.

'Are you good skiers?' Asta's husband asked.

'Binnab isn't. If we meet the Kiralas in the forest, we'll be captured.'

'The whole shore is free of snow. You can walk there,' said Asta.

'If we meet the Kiralas on the shore, then we'll be captured, too. And I don't wish to fight any more. I want to go home.'

'Then you'll have to risk the ice route after all.'

At dusk, they left together with Asta's husband and two brothers-in-law. Tulle and Binnab had been supplied with a flat-bottomed iceboat with a double keel, that could be drawn like a sledge. Asta had packed food and kindling into it, so they would not have to waste time hunting on their way. She had also given them high sealskin shoes that had been smeared with blubber to make them watertight, together with wooden spikes to tie under them.

Tulle was glad of his escort. Here where the islands were plentiful, the ice had been melted by the sun in many places and was uncertain, so the shortest routes westwards were not always the best. In some of the narrows, swift currents ran below the ice, and the rising water had been pressed up, so they went up to their knees through the new ice and they had to look out for hidden open channels. The men walked widely separated, joined together by long ropes, and thrusting their spears into the ice ahead of them.

Asta's husband halted beyond the last wooded islands and pointed out the direction of their journey. 'Follow the Plough until midnight, then the Magnificent. Keep the North Star on your right – but you know that, of course. And the Red Star should be ahead of you.'

'The Red Star was burning when I was born,' said Tulle. 'And it was burning again when I built my country.'

He and Binnab bade farewell to their companions and went on westwards alone.

All one day, then another, they were on their way. Then a third – it was as if the distance had grown longer since they had been riding with Bork. They skied using their spears as ski-sticks, hauling the ice-boat along behind them on a rope. The first night they saw firelight on the coast and guessed it was the Kiralas. They heard wolves too, and guessed the wolves were out hunting seals. The moon crossed their tracks and glided northwards, growing larger and more brilliant. They came to fields of broken ice and had to make a detour. They came to open channels that they crossed by boat. They walked every night and as far as they could into the morning, until the sun was high and the melting ice gurgled all round them, the snow sticking to their skis so thickly that they could move only with very small steps. During the day, they camped on an island, sleeping in the boat to keep dry, waking now and again to shift it into the shade.

On the fourth day, gulls flew over them and Tulle was uneasy, as this meant open water. He climbed up on to the next island they came to and searched the horizon. Yes, there were dark strips to the south, and a flutter of white birds against the darkness, as well as a ringing note that died away in the wind, but kept coming back again and again – the call of the long-tailed duck – they had come. 'We must hurry,' he said to Binnab.

He was afraid that they had gone too far out. He was also afraid that they had gone too far west. They struggled towards the coast as fast as they could, sweating under the rising sun. The snow was so wet now that it did not stick any longer, but turned into blackish-grey pools behind them at every step. The wind was against them. They chewed on dried meat as they walked, giving themselves no time to rest. Towards midday, they saw a small island Tulle recognized. It was called the Cormorant, and from the top of it, Tuntula Beacon Mountain could just be seen in the north-west. They went on despite their fatigue, slipping about in their sealskin shoes, despite the spikes. They had abandoned their skis, now.

But it was strange. However much they hastened, the Cormorant came no closer, and now they could hear the constant sound of waves hissing and splashing. Tulle stopped, telling Binnab to climb up on to his shoulders and look about. There was open water in front of them as well. The whole ice-field was drifting. Along the edge of the ice ran a wall of crushed floes, flung higher and higher, white in the sunlight, making it impossible to launch the boat.

There was no point in hurrying. They sat down to get their breath back and had some food.

They drifted for a day, then another, then a third. They floated past rock isles where the ice was crushed and flung up into heaps. They heard seal-pups whining and whimpering and large seals roaring. Birds swung above them, more and more each day. They were drifting on a raft of whitish-green ice across blue-black water, the sun leaping out like a beast of prey, red and

greedy every morning, the ice-floes wearing away, grinding against each other, dissolving into slush.

They got into the boat when the floe no longer bore them, expecting every minute to be crushed between the heaving floes. They were carried landwards, where there were long sandy shores, but before they reached them, the wind turned and carried them northwards again. The mist came down, their food came to an end, and it was difficult until they managed to kill a seal-pup on an ice-floe. The drank its blood, but they couldn't decide – should they offer the flesh to the Lord of the Sea? Or should they do the opposite, hide from him that they had killed one of his children?

They had to be on their guard all the time, using oars and spears against the ice-floes, pushing them away, fending them off, poling away. They heard the sound of the breakers in the mist, rowed towards it and went ashore on an island. They hauled the boat high up on land, collapsed beside it and slept.

When they woke they searched for driftwood and lit a fire. The old iron shield now showed goodwill towards them, allowing them to use it as a frying pan as they prepared the flesh of the seal. After each meal, Tulle scoured it thoroughly and thanked it.

The second time it showed goodwill towards them was when after days of waiting with clear views and open water, and days of uncertain sailing and laborious rowing, they came to the waters outside Tuntula. The wind was blustery, and the sail, made from Tulle's cloak, split and fell overboard. Tulle managed to hold the boat with the wind, but he could not move it forward. Binnab took the shield, now shinier than ever, and caught the sun in it, sending flash after flash towards the shore.

The sun was just setting, the clouds closing in and dusk swiftly falling. But an answering fire flared from the shore. Tulle was rowing with his back to the shore, but Binnab cried out that he had seen a longboat launched with a torch fastened to the pole in the prow.

The shield showed goodwill towards them for a third time and allowed them to use it as a fireplace. Tulle dared not stop rowing for a moment, but he told Binnab to whittle shavings off the spear shaft, the only wood they had, then set fire to them and if possible keep the fire going.

Binnab did so, crouching down at the bottom of the boat between Tulle's legs to get out of the wind, scorching his beard and burning his fingers, holding the little heap of shavings in place with his knife, so that the whole fire would not blow overboard.

The thunder of the storm and the waves was so loud that not even the loudest shout could be heard, but the men in the long-boat saw their little fire and came towards them. They flung over a rope with a chunk of wood on it and Binnab, who had scrambled past Tulle at the oars, fastened it to the prow. The boat was hauled in, eager hands helping first Binnab then Tulle over the railing of the long-boat.

The boat was the *Eider*, called that because she rode the water so lightly. Sixteen men rowed eight pairs of oars, Egil at the helm, grinning all over his face down at Tulle and Binnab lying on the bottom of the boat, numb with fatigue.

Someone cut off their wet and icy clothes, swept skins round them and gave them sucking-horns of ale to drink. Someone else also tried to prise open Tulle's fist. He had been grasping the shield so firmly that he could not unbend his fingers.

When he could speak again, he said: 'How is it you have the *Eider* in the water so early?'

'Libite advised it,' said Halva, who was crouching down beside him, struggling with his stiffened fingers.

'Is it you?' he said. But he was not surprised. 'You again.'

'Libite had Egil launch the *Eider* even before the ice melted – in a channel. She had them caulk and tar the hull. Some of them laughed, but no one opposed her. Perhaps I helped her a little. And day after day, night after night, she's had a lookout on Beacon Mountain, as well as on Rummel Island and Troll Island.'

'How is she?' said Tulle.

Halva put the narrow end of the horn between Tulle's lips again. 'She's well. Twins this time. Both boys. They're fine, too.'

The boat was rowed swiftly on, towing behind it the swinging little boat. They came to the narrows between Outer Mountain and Rummel Island, the wind dropping at each swing of the oars, the waves growing smaller. Then they came into the lee below the land. Tulle heaved himself up, groaning, his whole body aching, at the same time so numb he felt quite shapeless. Supported by strong little Halva, he raised his head above the railing.

There were several bonfires burning on the shore, the flames reflected in the water, and farthest out on the rocks, black against the firelight, stood Libite. The waves were insignificant here, as the wind was blowing offshore, but all the same both her foot and her paw were wet. She was holding up her long leather skirt in her hands.

# 14
# BINNAB'S SECOND TALE

The children of Tulaborg were very pleased to have Binnab back. They wanted stories from him, preferably immediately. At least one tale. As soon as he had recovered from his experiences and could walk and move again, they took him with them to their best places on the shore and among the rocks. They included him in their games and they made him sing. He had a way of drawing out the notes, trembling, whining, inhuman, until they shuddered and shivered and were forced to laugh. They invited him to banquets at which the food was all the small green new grass they could find, bitter buds, small shellfish, and water from a birch-bark cornet to drink.

One day they asked him: 'What's the most remarkable thing you've ever seen?'

He thought for a while, then answered: 'A door.'

'Was it of stone?' the children asked. 'Like the troll-door into the mountain? Was it of silver and gold? Or was it like the sun-door at Svipul's wedding, of such strong light that it's invisible but burns everyone who goes too close?'

'No,' said Binnab. 'The door I'm thinking of was of wood.'

'Wood?' said the children.

'It was carved,' said Binnab. 'It was covered all over with pictures. The tree of life, buds and cones and all kinds of leaves and birds and animals and tiny little creatures. The serpent in the earth and the Lord of the Skies at the top. The Lord of the Skies has sharp eyes and grasping claws, his wings hanging down along the edges of the door, feather by feather, on each side of the tree.'

'We've seen carved doors like that, too,' said the children. 'There's a man who lives in Ostankil here, and he can carve forest animals and hunters. He's going to carve picture boards for us to have in the hall.'

'The door I remember,' said Binnab, 'was not carved by men. It was made by birds that had pecked at it for many years.'

The children laughed with delight. 'That'd be fun to see,' they said. 'Sometimes in the spring, we stand watching the woodpecker drumming. But there are never any pictures, just holes where it's been.'

'The door I saw,' said Binnab, 'was made by pigeons. And pigeons have weak beaks. They can't even peck out nesting-holes for themselves.'

The children's eyes shone. 'Where did it lead to?' they asked.

'It led here,' said Binnab.

A town gradually grew up round Tulle's kingly

domain, a town called Tulavall, after the grazing pastures. It never grew large, but for many many years it was important.

King Tulle's name has been preserved throughout all its history, although the saga about him changed with time. For instance, it was said that on his homecoming, he turned himself into a seal and swam ashore with the frozen Binnab on his back. And Binnab, it was said, was a bird.